MW01658527

Eric,
Happy Gardening!
Janet Carson

Field to FEAST

YOUR YEAR-ROUND GUIDE TO GROWING YOUR OWN EDIBLE GARDEN IN ARKANSAS

Published by the Arkansas Democrat-Gazette
Arkansas' Largest Newspaper

Printed in the United States of America

Narrative by Janet Carson

Designed by Seth Massengill

Edited by CJ Gilbert

Coordinated by Amanda Copley

Contribution photos by Clay and Janet Carson

WEHCO Publishing
P.O. Box 2221
Little Rock, AR 72203

JANUARY

THE BEGINNING OF THE new year is a great time to take stock of how well your garden grew last year and make plans for this year. Good planning can be the difference between a good garden and a great garden. Take inventory of your garden now and consider how well it did last season. Start exploring your options and in the spring you can be ready to plant. What vegetables did well and which did you struggle with? What varieties did you like and what performed the best? Plot out your garden on paper and be ready for planting.

It's too early to plant early in the month, but in late January to early February we can start planting English peas and snow peas from seed. Vegetable transplants typically don't hit garden centers until mid- to late February. If you want to grow your own vegetable transplants, it takes 6 to 8 weeks to grow a quality transplant and you need either a greenhouse or artificial light to get optimal growth. New LED light kits can make that job much easier than in the past.

HARVEST

Bok Choy

Cabbage

If you planted a late fall/winter garden your vegetables should be growing well–from winter greens to broccoli, cabbage, bok choy and more. In mild winters they can grow unprotected with no damage but if temperatures are going to drop below 28 degrees, a light covering will help protect them. An inverted plant pot, cardboard box or a small covering will do the trick. With just a little extra work, you can harvest fresh vegetables all winter long.

Plant of the Month

Swiss Chard

Beta vulgaris

SWISS CHARD IS A KISSING COUSIN of beets, but it is grown for leaf production instead of root production. Instead of eating the fleshy roots–like in a beet plant–we eat the leaves and stems. Swiss chard is easy to grow and will last almost year-round in Arkansas, but it is particularly showy in the fall, winter and early spring garden because of its colorful stalks and large, glossy leaves. Edible landscaping is easily achieved with this plant.

The leafstalk (or petiole) can be a variety of colors including red, white, yellow or orange. Candy cane is a variety with red- and white-striped petioles. In the 19th century chefs often separated the mid-rib from the leaves and prepared it like asparagus. The leaves were dressed like spinach. Today, it is a commonly used vegetable in its own right, but it is also used as a substitute for spinach in most recipes. Both the foliage and the stalks are edible.

Although Swiss chard prefers cool weather, it does not bolt (or go to seed) as quickly as many other cool-season vegetables. The plant produces a small bulbous root, and if it is frozen back or cut for harvest, it can produce another set of leaves from the root system, which increases your harvest.

Q&A

Q. What, exactly, is arugula, and can it be grown in Arkansas?

A. Arugula is one of the new gourmet salad greens. It is also called rocket. It grows well in Arkansas and only slows down during the hottest summer months, when the greens can also become a bit more bitter tasting. Arugula has a spicy, almost peppery flavor to it and is found in many salad mixes.

Q. My daughter received a Kadota fig tree for Christmas. She loves figs and has difficulty finding them here in Fayetteville, hence the tree. What are the requirements for planting it in Northwest Arkansas, when and how does it thrive? Is there anything special that she must do for it to produce?

A. Growing figs in Northwest Arkansas is always a bit tricky. If you look at trends, they are saying the area is getting warmer and figs should overwinter fine. In central Arkansas, figs have gotten very winter hardy; however, that has not always been the case. In the 1980s, we called them fig bushes, because they froze back so often. In NWA, plant any variety in a more protected spot–giving it full morning sun and protection from cold winds. The Kadota fig is a green fig that is commercially grown in California and is supposedly the main fig used in Fig Newton cookies. It should be hardy in Northwest Arkansas but could be susceptible to hard freezes. Celeste and Brown Turkey are two figs we grow more commonly in Arkansas and would be a bit more hardy. The common fig does not need cross pollination, so it can produce figs with just one tree. They also bear on the current season growth. So even if winter damage does occur, it is possible to still have fruit.

Q. On the clay pots of my potted plants is a powder-like white substance on the outside, top of the pot (where the potting soil has not started yet) and sometimes a ring further down, towards the middle. (I even have a pot that has been empty for a while and the substance is still on it.) I have tried to wipe it off with alcohol, but it does not come off. How can I get rid of it and what could that be?

A. The white substance you see on the outside of your pots is accumulated salt. This salt comes from the fertilizers you are using and leaches through the containers. The potting soil you are using is pre-mixed with fertilizer, but it would happen from using any fertilizer in the containers. Soak the pots in a 10 percent diluted bleach and water bath and let them sit for 30 minutes to an hour. Then rinse thoroughly. If you still see the white substance, use a small brush to clean them and allow them to dry in the sunlight. It doesn't hurt the pots or the plants, but may not be the most aesthetically pleasing. This cleaning of the containers also sterilizes them and gives you a clean start for the growing season.

Q. I planted two Arkansas Black apple trees four years ago. They were in 3-gallon containers and about 5-feet tall. The trees are about 12 feet tall now, appear healthy, have never been pruned and have never bloomed. I fertilize each spring and fall. Will they ever produce or should I remove them and start with new trees?

A. Be patient. If you planted standard apple trees–not dwarfs–you may not have any apples until the trees are 8 to 10 years old. Dwarfs can begin fruiting at a younger age and are smaller trees. It seems your trees are growing nicely. They should be pruned every year in late February–whether they are fruiting or not. Be aware that apple trees need cross pollination–meaning they need a different variety of apples to bloom at the same time to share pollen. Plant a dwarf variety of another apple tree nearby to pollinate your Arkansas Black apple tree will.

Q. We have had a small backyard garden (20 feet by 50 feet) for many years. I put compost and fertilizer (10-20-10) on it every year. In the spring, I put on some well-composted chicken manure and till it into the soil. I rotate the crops around in this space, so as not to plant the same crop in the same space two years in a row. But, in the last two years, I have not been able to grow any radishes, turnips or similar root crops. All they produce is green tops. What can I put in the soil to cure this problem?

A. I assume you have ample sunlight, because all vegetables need a minimum of 6 to 8 hours of sunlight to produce. I think, possibly, the soil is too rich, putting loads of nitrogen into the foliage and not forming the roots. Try mixing some coarse sand into the planting area and using only a light application of a 10-10-10 fertilizer. Make sure you plant in the cool season (before April 15), thin the seedlings to give them ample room to grow and see what happens this year.

Q. I plant kale and rape in the spot that I will follow with tomatoes and corn. Are they a good cover crop that will add nutrients to the soil when tilled in or do I need to plant something else to improve the soil?

A. They should do great. You can also harvest from them before turning in the remains. Having a cover crop keeps weeds away. Other choices include vetch, rye, oats or turnips.

Q. For the last two years my son has used black plastic under his vegetables for weed control. I wanted to suggest pine straw to him, but I don't know what happens with pine straw as it breaks down. We plant tomatoes, okra, peppers and purple hull peas. What should I use in place of the black plastic?

A. Black plastic can be used in a vegetable garden and it does heat up the soil early, but can cause too much heat later in the season. If you are using plastic, you need to make sure there is a drip system or soaker hose under the plastic, or watering can be a real challenge. Pine straw is OK for a vegetable garden, but it is slower to break down than some mulches and will eventually make the soil more acidic. Shredded leaves, shredded paper and straw make great mulches and can easily be added back into the soil.

Q&A

Q. Please let me know the easiest way to winter blackberry plants that are in pots. They were dug up in early November and are sitting on my deck.

A. Blackberry plants are very winter-hardy, but in containers they would need a little protection. All containerized plants will be less winter-hardy than if they were in the ground. The root system is limited in the containers, plus the container is elevated so the soil temperature will get colder. Either group the plants and pots together and put some mulch around the base, or heel the pots into soil and mulch the tops. This will give you extra protection, should it get cold. If you know where you want them to grow, you could also plant them now.

Q. We moved from Ireland to Rogers a couple months ago and purchased a lovely family home with a large backyard. The backyard is currently lawn, with a couple of medium-sized trees and a few plant beds set away from the grass with low stone walls around the house. I used to be an active gardener in Ireland, but I am new to this area and don't know what grows well here and when to start planting. I am interested in planting some herbs and maybe some berries. I won't be able to spend very much time gardening though, as I have 1-year-old twins and they are a handful! Can you suggest some herbs and fruit plants for our new home?

A. Herbs are very easy to grow and you can do a variety of both annuals and perennials. For dry, sunny areas, consider the perennial rosemary and thyme. Oregano, fennel, garlic and sage are also very easy to grow. Cilantro is best grown in the fall as a winter annual. Parsley is a biennial and does well for a couple of seasons. Basil and dill are both summer annuals and thrive in Arkansas summers with a little bit of water. Blackberries and blueberries are both easy to grow and require little care, other than occasional pruning and water. Raspberries are a tad trickier, but they can be grown. As you have time, consider joining the Benton County Master Gardeners. They have a very active group of gardeners in your area. You will learn a lot and get to know fellow gardeners in your community.

Blackberry

Q. My husband is eager to prune our fig trees. I think you said to wait until February to do this. Please advise.

A. I think it is important to wait until late February before pruning, especially to prune your fig tree. If you prune it too early, you expose more of the plant to potential damage. Cold winters are not kind to fig trees and I would make sure they are out of the woods from winter weather before pruning. I don't think it is a bad idea to wait until March. Early pruning does expose more of the plant to winter injury, so tell him to be patient.

Q. My son has three potted lemon trees (or bushes). One he has had for three years and two for two years. The first year, the first tree was loaded with lemons. I suggested he cut it back in the winter. It reproduced this year, but not nearly as much. Neither of the newer trees produced as much as the first one had. During the summer they sit in full sun all day on the deck rail. I contend the pots should be placed deep in the ground to protect the root system from the heat. What say you?

A. Lemon trees like warm temperatures and should be fine outdoors unless the pot is small and overheating. You can sink the pots in the ground to aid in watering for the summer months, but they will put out roots into the surrounding soil which can make lifting them in the fall a bit more difficult. Lemons can be ever-bearing given the right conditions: enough sunlight (minimum 6 to 8 hours per day) and warm temperatures (at least above 60 degrees). That means they can continually bloom and have fruit in a variety of stages. I think the pruning job may have set them into a growing phase and cut back on some of the blooms. Prune minimally, but make sure there is room to house them indoors. Give them bright light, keep them watered and feed monthly while actively growing and they should rebound.

Q. We live in Walnut Ridge. We have five big pecan trees, all different varieties. One is a very good tree and the pecans are always good. Our question is, can we plant the pecans from this tree to grow more like it or do pecan trees have to be grafted to some other kind of plant?

A. Pecans do not breed true from seed. They cross pollinate to set fruit, so the resulting product, if grown from seed, may be similar or totally different. You actually need two different varieties of trees to get nuts. Planting a seed may give you something similar, or totally different, and it will take a good 7 to 10 years before you see a fruit. Grafting is by far the preferred method. Other good varieties to try include: Oconee, Pawnee, Desirable, Kanza or Lakota.

FEBRUARY

FEBRUARY IS PRUNING MONTH for many plants. Fruit trees, blueberry bushes and grape vines all need to be pruned every year. If you are a commercial grower and have hundreds of plants, you may need to start pruning earlier in the month. Most home gardeners, however, have a handful of plants and should wait to prune as late in the month as possible. Pruning early exposes your plants more and could lead to winter damage if extremely cold weather were to occur after pruning. We often see some early blooms on fruit trees this month, but don't worry, more will follow. Even if we lose a few blooms to a hard freeze, you can still have a full harvest. Clean up any debris that remains on the trees or around them. Starting the season off as clean as possible is the best way to prevent problems.

This is also the season to plant new fruit trees and blueberry bushes. Most nurseries carry the most varieties now. Be aware that most fruit crops benefit or need a plant to cross-pollinate with. Also remember, most tree fruits are not carefree–they do need spray programs and annual pruning.

If your soil is workable, now is the time to start planting cool-season vegetables. We can start with English and snow peas, then plant spinach, cabbage, broccoli, kale and more. Broccoli, cabbage, Brussels sprouts and cauliflower should be planted by transplant (small plants), while peas, spinach, carrots and lettuce can be planted by seed. Onions are planted either as sets or transplants, rarely from seed.

HARVEST

If you have a winter garden, you should be harvesting. Many gardeners are now growing year-round, and occasionally need to cover their plants to protect them from a hard freeze. If your plants go through a wide array of temperatures or we have a mild winter, the plants may bolt early. Bolting is when they send up a flower stalk. Fluctuations in temperature are to blame for this. You can't stop it once it starts, but try to use the vegetables you have before they go to seed.

The soil is the foundation of a garden. The healthier the soil, the more resilient your plants will be. Too many of us in Arkansas are blessed with more rocks than soil, but even those who have decent soil often lack organic matter. Building up a strong soil and amending with organic matter in the form of compost gives plants a better start in life and makes them easier to maintain. When amending soil, it is best to blend in your amendments with the existing soil. Creating a homogenous mix, rather than layering in different soil types, will encourage better rooting. While fall is an excellent time to test your soil to determine the pH and nutrient levels, you can still test the soil now. To test your soil, take slices of soil from the surface down around 6 inches. Get soil from 6 to 10 different spots in your yard or garden for each sample you are taking. Mix it together and take one pint of soil for each sample into your local county extension office. Within two to three weeks you will get a computer printout mailed to you with the results and recommendations on what to do.

One of the most important numbers on your soil test report is the pH of the soil. PH is a measurement of the acidity or alkalinity of the soil. It is measured in a range of zero to 14. While 7 is considered neutral, below 7 is acid and above 7 is alkaline. Most plants like a slightly acidic soil, between 6 to 6.5. Blueberries and azaleas like soil to be even more acidic, getting in the range of 5 to 5.5. Many soils in Arkansas are acidic and we occasionally need to add lime to raise the pH. Lime that can be mixed into the soil will give quicker results than lime that is laid on the soil surface.

Plant of the Month

Kale

Brassica Oleracea

FOR YEARS, GROCERY STORES threw away kale that withered on the shelf. It was not the hot commodity that it is today. Kale is one of the superfoods, ranked among the top 10 of the world's healthiest foods when it comes to providing the most nutritional value for the fewest calories. Kale is loaded with antioxidants and vitamin C–a cup of kale contains more vitamin C than an orange.

Kale is in the cabbage family and is quite cold-hardy. It is easy to grow from seed, but is also sold as transplants. If you don't have any in your garden, this is the month to begin planting. Kale varieties come with green or purple, smooth or flat leaves. Some of the more popular varieties include dinosaur or Lacinato kale–which is also called Tuscan or black kale. This smooth-leafed kale has thin, upright, dark-bluish-gray foliage. It is considered sweeter than some of the other kales. Another kale, redbor, is not only nutritious, but quite showy in the winter garden. The foliage is purplish-red and gets darker as it ages. Regardless of which variety you are growing, give it full sun and even moisture and you will be rewarded with months of tasty leaves.

Q&A

Q. I have an established asparagus patch that I have had for several years. I normally quit harvesting on June 1 every year. I have done this in the past in another state and I would like to know if this is correct for Arkansas. Also, is it OK to treat with salt to keep the grass down, and when is the proper time to do this treatment?

A. I don't usually give a date to stop harvesting. You will usually harvest for 6 to 8 weeks, but really strong plants can produce longer. The key is to stop harvesting when the spears are smaller than a pencil in diameter. If you continue to harvest as the spears get smaller, you can deplete the energy of the plant, resulting in weaker harvests in years to come. Salt is an old-fashioned remedy for weed control in asparagus beds. Asparagus is more tolerant of salt than most other vegetables, but I hesitate to recommend it. Salt stays in the soil for a long time and can build up if you use it every year. If there is any slope in your garden the salt can leach into surrounding soil where other vegetables are less tolerant. I would suggest light cultivation and mulching to keep grass and weeds out.

Q. When is the best time to plant cauliflower, broccoli and Brussels sprouts? I have my garden tilled up and need to know when to plant these.

A. As soon as you can find vegetable transplants, you can plant. They usually don't start hitting the garden centers and nurseries until mid-February. All of the vegetables you named are usually grown from small transplants, versus seeds. Right now you can plant seeds for carrots, English peas, snow peas, spinach and greens. Just pay attention to the weather in case we get any more winter weather. Covering the plants with inverted containers or row covers can give them all the protection they need.

Q. We are thinking about creating raised beds for our vegetables this year. Does using treated timber create any unwanted chemical leaching into our vegetables? If so, what would you suggest is the best material for this project.

A. This is a topic that has been hotly debated for a while now. Studies have shown that chemicals from treated lumber don't leach into the plants, but many are skeptical. One way to build permanent raised beds would be to use products that are made from recycled materials. There are several brands of this plastic wood, and they look great and last forever. It may cost more on the front end, but it is basically maintenance free. At the People's Garden in Washington, D.C., the Urban Forestry Administration provided logs from locust trees, which decay more slowly in soil than most trees, and red oaks. They were not treated.

Q. I saved some seeds from some tomatoes I grew last season that we just loved. I am attempting to grow the plants for this year's garden. I have started with fresh soil and trays and have them in a very bright, sunny window, but the seedlings look so weak. Do they need fertilizer? If so, what kind and how much?

A. Even when we think we have enough sunlight with a regular window to grow transplants, the duration and strength of the light is not enough, unless you have a greenhouse window and full sun. Your plants are weak or leggy from low light. Rig up a light kit over the seedlings and leave it on for 12 hours per day. They now make light kits for home gardeners that contain LED lights, but you can also use an inexpensive shop light kit and adjust the height. A mild solution of a water-soluble fertilizer will help, but I really think low light is the culprit. Make sure you thin the seedlings out if they are too close together and don't be too quick to plant outdoors in the spring. Make sure the soil temperature warms up as well as the air temperature.

Q. I moved from Kansas to Arkansas a couple of years ago and am curious: What is our planting zone?

A. It depends on which USDA Hardiness Zone map you are using to determine what zone Arkansas is in. In the older version, which is still used by many gardening books and catalogs, Northwest Arkansas was zone 6 (average winter low temperature -10 to 0 degrees celsius), the central part of the state was zone 7 (0 to 10 degrees) and the southern tip was zone 8 (10 to 20 degrees for the average low temperature). The USDA came out with a new zone map after years of milder temperatures in 2012. The southern third of the state is now zone 8a (10 to 15 degree low) with the next tier moving north zone 7b (5 to 10 degrees) and the next third of the state is 7a (0 to 5 degrees). Keep in mind, the only piece of information you get from a zone map is the average low winter temperature–not summer temps, rainfall, humidity, etc. So don't use the Hardiness Zone map as your Bible when choosing plants. It just gives you some guidelines.

Q. I realize that our climate is warm for growing currants, but I would love to have some and wonder if you know how they have fared in our state. I am right between zone 7 and 8, in El Dorado.

A. Currants are in the Ribes genus. The common edible red currants really don't thrive in the heat of Arkansas summers. However, the clove currant, or Ribes odoratum, does pretty well in our gardens and has fragrant yellow flowers in the spring, followed by small black edible fruits in the summer. While not a prolific berry producer, and a bit gangly with age, it can give you some fruit. As far south as you are in El Dorado, it would be a challenge to grow the more common edible currants.

Q&A

Q. Can you tell us the name of a fruit tree spray that would work for nectarines, peaches and Italian plums? Last year we had a lot of mold on our fruit and we would like to do a better job this year.

A. Your best bet is to look for a complete home fruit orchard spray. Many brand names are available. Be sure to read the label and make sure it says it is for diseases and insects, since you need both insecticides and fungicides to have clean fruit. Having it pre-mixed makes it easier. Begin the spray schedule when two-thirds of the flower petals fall and repeat every 2 to 3 weeks throughout the season.

Q. I have a key lime tree, which I grew from seed. It is about 5 feet tall and bloomed profusely for the first time this year. Unfortunately, my tree has been attacked by insects that I believe to be scale. I went to the nursery to find something to get rid of the scale and the proprietor told me there was really nothing that would be effective on citrus. I am guessing that a systemic insecticide would be necessary to kill them. Is there something you would suggest? If I treat my lime tree with such an insecticide, could we eat the fruit in future years?

A. Unless the product is labeled for edible plants, don't use it. There are some formulations of insecticides for fruit trees. Probably your best bet now would be horticultural oil. You need to have thorough coverage for the product to be effective and smother out the insects. Once the scale insects die, they won't fall off. But, you should see the plant gaining in vigor, and no new insects. There are several formulations–dormant oil is heavier, while some of the sun spray oils are more refined and can be used on plants that are not dormant. You may want to wait until you can move the plant outside before spraying. Avoid using the products when it is extremely hot.

Q. I moved into a new house last year and it has grape vines along a back trellis. I saw a cluster or two of grapes last summer, but we spent our time getting moved in so I basically ignored the yard. I would like to know how and when to prune the grape vines and what other care they might need.

A. Grapes should be pruned annually in February. Since you probably don't know how old the plants are, you will need to judge the severity of pruning by the vigor of the plants. With table grapes, we count buds when pruning. Count buds on the arms or branches that fan out from the main trunk. Older, well-established and vigorous plants can have up to a total of 60 buds left on them, while young plants may only have 10 buds remaining after pruning. You may think you are killing the plants by how much you are taking off, but keep in mind that each bud can produce one or two clusters of grapes. If you leave too many buds, the plant may not be able to support them all and the resulting grapes may ripen one grape at a time. Many grape vines also require a thorough spray program to combat insects and diseases.

Q. I received a packet of tomato seeds with a catalog order. Is it possible to grow your own transplants from seeds without a greenhouse? If so, how would I do it?

A. Growing your own transplants can be done, but you need to provide an artificial light source. Typically, the biggest drawback to growing your own transplants is insufficient light. You cannot grow quality transplants in a sunny window. Rig up an artificial light source within 6 to 8 inches of the soil. Leave the light source on for a minimum of 10 to 12 hours per day. Keep the seedlings moist, but allow them to dry out slightly in between watering. Use a water-soluble fertilizer as they begin to grow. It typically takes a minimum of 6 to 8 weeks to grow a transplant large enough to move outside. You may find it is much easier to simply buy transplants than growing your own. The only advantage to growing your own is better variety.

Q. When is it time to trim peach trees? I haven't pruned in a few years and I need to prune back quite a bit.

A. All fruit trees should be pruned every year. While commercial growers begin pruning much earlier, home gardeners have a bit more flexibility since they have only a few trees to prune. Prune any time from late February up until the trees begin to bloom. Pruning before blooming is optimal. If you don't prune annually, you will typically have a lot of small fruit versus nice, large fruits.

Peach tree

MARCH

Lettuce

Planting potatoes

GARDENING SEASON is in full swing. When we have a mild winter, gardens grow quicker and gardeners get a bit overzealous and want to plant too early, but try to use common sense. While it is time to plant the cool-season vegetables, including cabbage, spinach, lettuce, broccoli, potatoes, carrots and onions, it is NOT time to plant tomatoes. Regardless how warm the days are, we are not out of the woods on a frost and you should not plant warm-season vegetables until, at the earliest, mid-April. Unless you have a greenhouse, don't buy them.

One of the most common things I hear from novice or non-gardeners is that they don't have a green thumb and everything they plant dies. I think a lot of that comes down to the wrong plant for the wrong place or planting in the wrong season. It is imperative that garden centers and nurseries sell the right plants for the right planting season. If a new gardener goes to a garden center and sees a tomato plant now, the message is "it is time to plant tomatoes." And it is NOT. I think we all need to rally together and make sure that what we sell will grow when we sell it or where it will be planted. We need to do all we can to make gardeners successful.

HARVEST

It all depends on how cold our winter gets as to whether we have damage on our fig trees. Folks in central and southern Arkansas aren't bothered too often by winter damage, but in really cold years, many figs struggle. We are not totally out of the woods in early March, but we can all hope that cold winter weather is over. When plants are begin to break dormancy and grow is when they are often the most susceptible to a late frost. Covering with sheets, inverted boxes or flower pots can give you a few degrees of protection. Small plants are easy to cover, but for fruit trees, you usually have to do a Hail Mary and hope for the best. Avoid the use of plastic unless you have air space between the plastic and the plants. Plastic covering generates extra heat and condensation builds up under it. This moisture freezes at night and the added fluctuation in temperature can wreak havoc on many plants.

Early spring is one of the easiest times to grow vegetables. You tend to have more energy in the spring, and we often have ample moisture. Diseases and insects haven't gotten firmly entrenched, either. So, grab your shovel and start planting. If you don't have space for a large garden, plant some vegetables in pots or in amongst your flowers. A minimum of 6 hours of sunlight is all you need.

Broccoli, cabbage and cauliflower are usually grown from transplants–not seed-sown this late. Onions can be started from sets or transplants, but rarely seeds. Transplants are usually the most common method. Most

Cabbage

feed stores carry them in bundles of small plants, which are then set out in the garden. Plant them 2 inches apart, and as they grow, use every other plant for green onions, giving the remaining onions plenty of room. Onion sets are small, dry onions that are often bundled in a bag. Try to pick sets that are smaller than a dime in diameter. The larger sets tend to bolt and go to seed before setting a big onion. They can be used for green onions. Remember to fertilize at planting and then side-dress 6 weeks later.

Sugar snap peas

Greens, spinach, beets, lettuce, English and sugar snap peas are all planted by seed, and potatoes are normally started from seed potatoes. Broadcast fertilizer at planting, and side-dress 6 weeks later. Mulch the plants, water as needed and wait. Monitor the garden periodically, but you don't have to be as diligent now as you do when all the pests kick in.

Let's all keep our fingers crossed that this is going to be a fantastic gardening season. Edible gardening has been increasing in popularity for the past 5 years, and that trend has not slowed down. If new gardeners start gardening in a horrid weather year, they may get discouraged. Don't let one bad season slow you down. Try, try, try again.

Plant of the Month

Asparagus

Asparagus Officinalis

It is asparagus season. Asparagus is a wonderful perennial vegetable that can easily be grown in the home garden. Asparagus likes a well-drained soil in full sun and it prefers a rich soil. Work some well-rotted manure or compost into the soil. Plant your 1-year-old asparagus crowns in a stand-alone garden or to the north side of your vegetable bed. You want to have them in an easily accessible area, but not in the middle of your ongoing garden, as the fronds in the summer tend to get tall. Asparagus is a dioecious vegetable, meaning there are separate male and female plants. Some gardeners prefer to plant all male plants, including the

Jersey series: Jersey giant, Jersey gem, Jersey knight, Jersey supreme and the UC157. While others do a mix of males and females, including the Mary and Martha Washington types. Females tend to be less productive, but produce larger spears. Often, we plant what is available at our local outlets.

Dig a trench about 9 to 12 inches deep and about 4 to 6 inches wide, or as wide as the spread of the roots on the crowns you buy, and plant them with the crown up and roots spread out. Cover them with about 2 inches of soil. As the plants begin to grow above the soil line, continue to lightly cover with soil until the plants are at the original soil height. Water as needed throughout the first year, and keep weeds in check. Asparagus crowns must be 3 years-old before harvesting. If you harvest them when the plants are getting established in the first 2 years, you will be taking energy away from the roots, which can impact the harvest for the life of the plants. Once the plants are 3 years old, you can harvest for about 2 to 3 weeks the first season. Harvest the spears when they are 4 to 8 inches long. Stop harvesting when the spears get smaller than a pencil in diameter. Fresh asparagus from the garden is a treat, and although it can be stored for about 3 weeks in the refrigerator, the longer you store it the more the sugar content declines.

Q & A

Pomegranate blooms

Q. I am interested in growing ornamental pomegranates in my yard Where I can obtain some and what is the best kind to get? If they are good for birds to eat, then I want the fruiting kind; if not, then I want the flowering kind.

A. I don't know if birds eat them or not, but they sure are pretty. Punica granatum is the plant in question and there are numerous varieties. Most produce bright orange flowers, although there are cultivars with white and pink flowers. I like the bright orange. Fruit can vary from small reddish fruits to the large ones seen in grocery stores. Granada is the hardiest of the pomegranates, and it does set fruit. Most are only reliably winter-hardy through central Arkansas but I am seeing them growing farther north all the time. As for availability, check with your local nursery and see if they can get it for you. Pomegranates are becoming much more accessible.

Q. When I plant my tomatoes in the ground, they start out pretty good for the first 2 weeks. Then, when they start coming up, during the next 2 weeks, they start drying out. After blooming and producing the tomato, the same problem is occurring. As the blooms come out they will dry and fall off. Needless to say, the tomatos plants have a short life span. They will totally stop producing around mid-summer. I was told that I was probably splashing water up on the plants too much when watering. Last year I only had a soaker hose on them. I put straw down around the bottom of the plants, but to no avail. Maybe there is a better method that you can help me with.

A. First, get your soil tested. Take a pint of soil to your local county extension office and see what the pH is and the levels of N, P and K. I always want to start with the foundation of the plants, which is the soil. If your soil is pitiful and rocky, you can enrich it with compost. How is the drainage? If they are sitting in waterlogged soil, they will die quickly. We recommend that you rotate where you plant your tomatoes every year because many tomato diseases are soil-borne and attack the plants earlier each season. Having a problem beginning within 2 weeks of planting, though, is pretty amazing. I think we might have something else going on. Mulching the plants to keep soil from splashing on the stems can slow down the disease spread, but again, it doesn't usually occur within 2 weeks of planting, nor does it cause the flowers to dry. Most tomato diseases either start with the leaves dying from the bottom and it progresses up the stem, or we have a dramatic wilting and dying from one of the vascular wilts. It sounds like your problem is more about fruit set than plants dying. How much sunlight do the plants get? They need at least 6 hours per day. Some varieties quit setting fruit when the temperatures get above 90 degrees during the day or stay above 75 degrees at night, but if the plants look good, they can kick back in and produce well into fall. I think we need to investigate further. If the problem happens again, take in a plant sample this summer to your county extension office and let them send it to the diagnostic lab.

Q. I have a scuppernong vine that has gotten out of control. I was recently told to cut the vine down to the ground and let it restart. This seemed a little extreme, and I am not sure I would be brave enough to do this to mine. What are your thoughts on this advice?

A. Is it producing well? If it is, then there is room to salvage it. Scuppernongs are a type of muscadine grape and they can be quite prolific. You also need a male and a female plant to get fruit. I would try to prune it back by one-third to one-half and try to keep it pruned to a trellis or fence. If left to its own devices, it can grow up into your trees and all over your landscape. Growing in the shade of a large tree can cut down on its production. It will produce much better in full sun. Make sure to prune annually to keep it growing and producing to its full potential.

Q. I am planning my summer vegetable garden and trying to figure out what type of irrigation system I want to use. I have been told not to get the plant itself wet when watering tomato plants. Is this true? If so, why? Would drip irrigation be better than overhead?

A. Tomatoes are plagued with a whole range of plant diseases. Many of these diseases are soil-borne and water splashing from the ground to the stems can help increase their spread. Also, wet foliage, especially late in the day, can be a precursor to

Muscadine vine

Q & A

many disease issues. If you have ever taken a plant pathology course, there are three things in the disease triangle that must be present for a disease to take over: a susceptible host plant, the disease pathogen and climatic conditions necessary for the disease. Keeping the foliage dry can reduce disease spread if there are pathogens present, and if you are using any type of pesticide sprays, you don't wash them off as quickly. Drip irrigation is better than overhead watering for several reasons. It keeps the foliage drier, directs water to the root zone and is much more efficient.

Q. We are planning our summer garden and always have problems with squash vine borers destroying our otherwise healthy, productive summer squash and zucchini plants. Our only recourse seems to be replanting and hoping they don't attack the new plants. Is there a way to prevent such attacks?

A. While some squash vine borers may be overwintering in your garden to come back and attack, the adults seem to find even new squash plantings. There are two things you can do to help prevent injury. One is monitor for the adults, which look somewhat like a wasp with orange bodies. You can try trapping them–they are attracted to the color yellow. You can buy traps or make your own using a shallow pan of water painted yellow–an old plastic yellow butter tub works well. They will fly in and drown. When you see the adults, you can use an insecticide at the soil line, but it will need replenishing when washed off, and you need to be careful not to hurt your pollinators. If you plant using transplants, you can lightly wrap the stems that go into the ground with aluminum foil to act as a barrier to the boring larvae. If grown from seed, pull back the soil and lightly wrap the exposed trunk with foil, once it's established. One positive note is that we usually only have one generation of squash vine borers per year, so late plantings are usually not affected.

Q. I have a peach and a plum tree (plus a small plum tree for pollination.) The peach tree was, from the beginning, infected with what I think is Monilinia. The fruits look great at first but rot on the tree, with white fungal growths on the affected parts. By November, the trees are full of fruit "mummies." I have tried to collect and burn the "mummies" but it did not help much. I will have to spray, but how, and with what? Are there companies spraying fruit trees in Fayetteville, where I live? I will have to remove my trees (about 7 years old) unless I can fix this problem.

A. Brown rot of peaches, Monilinia fructicola, is a devastating problem and one of the reasons it is hard for home gardeners to grow peaches.

You think you are about to harvest a beautiful crop of peaches and then seemingly overnight they rot and turn to mush! Removing the mummies is important, since they are loaded with disease spores. Using dormant oil in the fall when the leaves drop and then again before they begin to break dormancy can help start the season clean, but it will not prevent the problem from occurring during the growing season. I do not know of any companies who spray home fruit trees, but you can do it yourself. Most nurseries carry a home fruit orchard spray, which contains an insecticide and fungicide. The downside is that it takes frequent applications to keep the trees clean. I think it is a lot easier to leave the peach-growing to the farmers and buy them at the farmer's market.

Q. My father, who lives in Kansas City, Missouri, has three Concord grape plants he wants me to have (passed on from his father). When should I attempt to move these plants to Arkansas? I live in Bella Vista. How close to the lake can I plant without worrying about the occasional flooding harming the roots? Also preparing our rocky soil has me worried. I know lime applications are called for but is that just when first transplanting? Thank you for any help, I'm definitely out of my comfort zone with grapes!

A. If your soil is extremely rocky, consider building a raised bed to plant them in along with a trellis for them to grow on. This will also alleviate any flooding problems. Have your soil tested before adding lime. Lime is only needed, if your soil is too acidic. Liming without knowing the amounts needed, can cause damage. Make sure that where you plant the grapes, they get a minimum of six hours of sunlight. I would move the plants soon, before they begin active growth. Late February to early March is the time to prune grape vines, so prune and move at the same time. They do need annual pruning as well.

APRIL

Lettuce

Lavender

APRIL IS A GREAT MONTH in the vegetable garden, allowing you to plant both spectrums of vegetables: the cool-season ones until mid-month, and the warm-season ones starting mid-month. This is the time of year that we need to pay attention to the weather. Late cold snaps are not unheard of, and some parts of the state have had rare April snows. (Let's hope that doesn't happen, but be prepared if it does.) If some of you jumped the gun and planted your tomatoes and basil too early, did not cover them and it got cold, go buy some new plants. It is usually best to wait until the middle of April before planting warm-season plants, but there are plenty of things you can plant now.

Until mid-month you can still plant all the cool-season vegetables including lettuce, broccoli, onions, greens and radishes. You can begin to plant green beans and corn; then add in tomatoes, squash, peppers and eggplants by mid- to late April. If you allow the soil to warm up, the warm-season plants will take off and produce much better than if you plant in cool soil. Even if we don't get a late-season frost (and we are keeping our fingers crossed that we won't), we still have cool nights, so be patient. When purchasing tomato plants, choose healthy plants in varieties you like, but remove any blooms or small fruits, if the seedlings have any. If your tomato plants begin setting fruit at a young age, all of the energy will go into fruiting and less into establishing a healthy, vigorous plant. While you may claim the title of first tomato in the neighborhood, overall your production will be lower.

You'll need to wait until May to plant southern peas, okra and sweet potatoes, but there is still plenty to do in the garden. Mix in compost to your garden beds, and broadcast a complete fertilizer at planting. Mulch the garden to keep weeds at bay, to conserve soil moisture and to moderate soil temperature. Start monitoring for pests now, too. Our plants grow faster in warmer weather, and so do insects and diseases. The sooner you can spot a problem, the quicker you can control it.

HARVEST

IF YOU PLANTED A LATE-FALL or early-winter vegetable garden, you are probably harvesting a good amount of lettuce, peas, spinach, broccoli and the like. As you harvest, replant in those spots with more vegetables. If our winter had a lot of fluctuating temperatures, some of the early vegetables can bolt or go to seed early. When they begin to produce a flower stalk, their season is over, so make the most of the harvest. Rotating crops will improve your chances of healthy plants. If you don't have your own homegrown produce, most farmer's markets start in April, so supplement until your crops start producing.

Herbs are also a great edible addition to the vegetable garden or the flowerbed. Some of the perennial herb plants can get nipped in abnormally cold winter weather, so inspect them as they begin growing to see if they need pruning or replacing. Now is a great time to start planting the warm-season annual herbs including basil and dill. Whether you grow them in the ground or in a pot, they are a great addition to the landscape, as well as the kitchen!

If you have pear or apple trees, monitor them for fireblight. Fireblight is a bacterial disease that is spread by pollinators during the blooming season. It first appears as black leaves on the tips of the branches. The ends of the, branches flag over, giving the appearance of a shepherd's crook. Sprays are rarely effective, and even if they do offer help, it is only during the blooming period, which is well past. For now, simply prune out any damage 6 to 8 inches back from where you see it. Be sure to sterilize your pruning shears in a Clorox or alcohol solution between cuts so you don't spread the disease from branch to branch mechanically. If you follow a spray schedule for tree fruits to keep the fruits clean of insects and diseases, you should be doing so. We normally start when two-thirds of the flower petals have fallen.

Strawberry

Strawberry season has started. If a late freeze hits your first flowers, you should still have strawberries, but the fruit from the first blooms is always the biggest. The central first flower on each plant is the king flower and produces the largest berries. It doesn't mean berry set is gone, but your resulting harvest may be a bit smaller. Don't fertilize strawberries until they have finished producing for the year. Early applications of nitrogen can lead to excessive foliage growth, which can result in more fruit rot during moist springs. Renovate your plantings by thinning them after harvest and then fertilize.

Plant of the Month

Onions

Allium cepa

Onions are easy vegetables to grow in the garden because they can be eaten at a variety of stages. They can be planted from February through mid-April. Onions are classified as short-day onions or long-day onions. Typically we do better in the south with short-day onions, which can begin producing a bulb before the days get longer and the temperatures hotter.

Onions are most commonly grown from sets or transplants. Sets are the bags of small onion bulbs you see in nurseries and garden centers. They are usually sold as red, white or yellow. Sets or bulbs that are larger than a dime in diameter will usually not produce large dried onions, but can be used

for green onions or small onions. Those that are smaller than a dime usually won't bolt as easily (meaning they will not send up a flower stalk), and will usually produce larger bulbs that can be stored longer.

All onions like good nutrition. Broadcast fertilizer into the bed at planting and side-dress every 2 to 3 weeks until close to harvest. Keep the plants watered and mulched.

The size of the onion bulb is related to the number and size of the green leaves at the time the bulb matures. If your bulbs can complete their life cycle without producing a flower stalk, the onions can be stored for months. An onion is a biennial, which means the first season it produces foliage, and the second season it blooms, sets seeds and dies. Fluctuating temperatures cause plants to bolt or flower prematurely.

Once you see a flower stalk appearing on your onions, it is time to harvest. Some people think they can cut the flower off and the bulb will continue to grow, but that won't happen–the flower stalk is coming up through the center of the bulb, and that can't be reversed. The resulting onion won't store as a dried onion, so harvest and plan to use them fairly soon. If your onion plants don't bolt, it is time to harvest when the foliage begins to die back or flop over. These onions can be stored in a cool, dry place and should last for months.

Any of the onion varieties or types can be used as green onions when the foliage is at least 6 inches high. If you like mild onion flavor, use your green onions when they are small. The larger they get, the stronger the flavor becomes.

Q & A

Q. I was given a beautiful bean called "Anasazi," a dark brown and white speckled bean, which when cooked looks like a light pinto bean, but very flavorful. My question is: Can I raise them? I am going to plant some and see if they germinate. Any info you can give me will be deeply appreciated.

A. The Anasazi bean is a dry bean that historically was grown by the Anasazis of the Four Corners region of the southwest. It is reported to be an ancient cultivar dating back more than 2,500 years. In the present, Adobe Milling Co. of Dove Creek, CO, holds the name as a registered trademark and beans with this seed-coat pattern cannot be sold under the name Anasazi unless authorized by Adobe Milling. But there are many other cultivars with similar maroon and white spotted seed-coat patterns and properties. These are: Jacob's Cattle, Trout Bean and Cave Bean, to name a few. These are usually harvested as dry beans, and this is the difficulty in growing them in Arkansas. You can grow them here, but not with the success that they have in Colorado where most are grown commercially. I would plant them as you would plant green beans or snap beans, but space the plants out to about two plants per row foot. Beans do not respond to heavy nitrogen fertilization, but need adequate amounts of phosphorus and potassium. Soil pH needs to be 6 or above. They can have all the same pests and disease as green beans, so monitor for problems.

It may take as long as 90 or more days to go to dry seed. You may wish to harvest the pods and shell out the seed and lay them out in your house to dry further. The seeds will store until the next year if kept below 50 percent relative humidity, and 50 degrees Fahrenheit.

Q. I have squash plants that have plenty of flowers but don't set any squash. I have seen bees in the yard, but not near the squash plants. Is there such a thing as male squash plants? Is there something I can do to get some squash?

A. Squash plants, like all members of the cucurbit family, have separate male flowers and separate female flowers. The flowers themselves look quite similar, but look behind the yellow blooms. On the male flower there will simply be a stalk, with the flowers containing stamens covered in pollen. The female flower will have a small squash behind the bloom hoping to get pollinated. If no bees come by to carry the pollen from the male bloom to the female bloom, you won't get any squash, unless you transfer the pollen manually by hand. Honeybees can be a bit finicky. If you only have a few squash blooms there may not be enough to interest them. They leave the hive and only travel to one type of bloom before heading back. If you have a handful of squash plants, they probably have more numerous blooms of other plants that they are attracted to.

Q. We had to give up a large landscaped house for a town house in Hot Springs Village. Therefore, I have grown tomato plants directly in bags of soil on a sunny deck (with slits in the bottom of the sacks). What tomato variety do you suggest as the very best? Peppers have been also successful, but what variety would you suggest as best? Has squash been successful?

A. You could ask 10 different gardeners which variety of tomato is best and you would probably get 10 different answers. We all have our favorites. Usually when we grow tomatoes in containers, which I would classify as the bag method, the bush type of tomato is easier to manage. Tomatoes come as either determinate varieties (bush type) or indeterminate (those that keep growing). The determinate ones usually have a stronger stem and don't require the rigid staking. They are usually more manageable in size, as well. For peppers, almost all should perform well. The banana-type peppers may not be as nutritionally needy as the bell-types, but with proper nutrition and watering, anything is possible. They sell space-saving varieties of squash and cucumbers–more bush-like in habit, specifically for containers. The key is a minimum of 6 hours of sunlight per day and ample moisture. Keep in mind, the more frequently you water, the more you will need to fertilize. Water-soluble or light applications of a granular fertilizer should work well.

Q. I'm looking for organic ways to control weeds around tomato plants. Is it okay to put mulch (i.e., cypress, hardwood, pine bark) around these plants? If so, is one type of mulch better than another?

A. I think all gardens should have mulch in them. Not only does it keep weeds down, mulch also maintains soil moisture levels, moderates soil temperature and prevents erosion. When using mulch in a vegetable garden, it is preferable to use something that can break down readily. The bark mulches can be used, but you would not want to till them into the soil at the end of the season. Shredded leaves, rice hulls, newspaper or shredded paper, or straw would be a better choice. Some gardeners do use plastic as a mulch in the vegetable garden, laying it down early to help warm the soil in the spring as well. Plastic is OK, but make sure you have a way to get water underneath it and possibly add some organic mulch on top to cool things down in the heat of summer.

Q. I would like to try growing a tomato plant in a pot this year. Are there any special techniques I should try? What about the soil? What mix should I use? This will be new for me, as I've grown Big Boy in the past, in a small sunny area in my back yard. I had the idea from a co-worker who has limited space because of apartment living.

A. Tomatoes are easy to grow in containers, but give yourself a break by planting them in large enough containers–that way they won't need constant water this

Q&A

summer. A minimum 5-gallon pot is best. Buy a commercial potting soil instead of using garden soil. Garden soil tends to be much heavier and can contain contaminates like weed seeds and insect larvae. If the site is in full sun, you may want to add some of water-absorbing polymers in with the soil to help it retain moisture. Some potting soils come with these already added, but regardless, don't get carried away with them–a little goes a long way. You can grow indeterminate varieties like Big Boy and use tomato stakes or cages just like in the garden, or you can grow the "patio" types which are really determinate varieties that have a stronger stem but limit the length of time you harvest. Fertilize at planting with a slow-release fertilizer, and then fertilize about every two weeks with a water soluble fertilizer. You will need to fertilize tomatoes grown in containers more often than those grown in the garden, because you are watering more often, since container soils dry out quicker due to smaller volume and elevated status. Watch for insects and diseases, but diseases are usually less of a problem because you are starting with fresh, sterile soil each season. Mulching the pot after planting will also aid in moisture retention. As with any tomato, give them a site that gets at least 6 to 8 hours of sunlight.

Q. I just relocated to Hot Springs Village this month from Dallas. I would like a recommendation of two or three types of tomatoes that can be grown in this area.

A. I think everyone has their particular favorite, but most varieties grow well in Arkansas. The key is to rotate where you plant them each season so diseases don't build up. In that vein, I would suggest you look for varieties that have V, F and N following their name. This means they are resistant to verticillium wilt, fusarium wilt and nematodes. Some popular varieties include Celebrity, Big Boy and Sweet 100 for a cherry type. One of my all-time favorites is the Pink Traveler 76 variety, but it is not always easy to find.

Q. I got a bit anxious this spring and planted my tomato plants in late March. I have covered them with milk jugs on every cool night and thought I had protected them from the several late frosts we had. The plants are still green, but they haven't grown a bit since I planted them. Do you think these plants will still produce, or should I replant?

A. You aren't alone in getting spring fever early. Tomatoes don't like cold soil or cool air temperatures, and may be sitting there waiting for both to warm up. To hedge all bets, plant a few extra plants nearby and see what happens. I don't like to begin planting tomatoes until mid- to late April, and see no problems even with May and June plantings.

Q. I am having difficulty with my fruit trees. Last year my peach tree produced lots of peaches, but they all dried up around the seed before they ripened. I also noticed that quite a few of the leaves and small branches dried up and died. My apple tree made really good apples but the leaves dried up and died and I noticed yellow spots on the leaves that had several round dots in them. I assumed these to be some kind of insect eggs. The apples also had dark spots

Peach tree

Apple tree

on them. I have already cut them back and am hoping that you can suggest some kind of spray, preferably something natural that I can use to solve these problems.

A. Fruit trees can be challenging for the home gardener, especially peaches, which have numerous insect and disease issues. Brown rot is the most destructive disease and can wipe out a crop seemingly overnight, especially when we have periods of rain close to harvest. Dry seasons are actually easier on peach growers than wet ones. Pruning is something you will need to do annually, but a spray schedule is also necessary to produce quality fruit. Purchase a home fruit spray that has both an insecticide and a fungicide mixed together. There are organic products as well as non-organic. Start spraying when two-thirds of the flower petals have fallen and then continue throughout the growing season, about every 10 days to 3 weeks depending on the weather. Your apple tree sounds like it was infested with cedar apple rust. This disease has 2 hosts: eastern red cedars and apple trees. By the time you see yellow spots rimmed in orange it is too late to spray to control it. The key is to do preventative sprays the first few weeks following bloom. Orange gelatinous masses form on cedar trees releasing spores which then infest the apples. Typically apple diseases are a bit easier to deal with since you can usually peel off the damage and still eat the fruit. Spray schedules, cultural information and pruning guides are available on our extension website at: www.uaex.edu/yard-garden/fruits-nuts/default.aspx.

MAY

Eggplant

Okra bloom

Watermelon

MAY IS A GREAT MONTH to plant vegetables. It is too late for the cool-season crops, but all of the warm-season crops can still be planted, from snap beans and corn to tomatoes, peppers, squash and eggplants. By May, our soil is warming up and we can begin to plant okra, southern peas, even watermelons and cantaloupes. Some of these plants take up a lot of space in the garden, so be sure to give them room to grow. Regular fertilization will give best production. Avoid too much fertilizer around the legumes (the beans and peas), but the other vegetables will benefit from regular nutrition and ample water. Mulching can help preserve moisture and keep weeds at bay. To keep the weeds from taking over, hoe or hand-weed regularly. Water your plants early in the day to allow the moisture to get into the soil before the heat builds up. You will lose less water to evaporation and help dry the foliage as quickly as possible. As temperatures heat up, so do pest problems. Monitor for insects and diseases to catch them early.

Full bloom squash

More gardeners are planting seeds than ever before. Seed sales have greatly increased, in both vegetable and flower seeds. When seeding, many gardeners get a little heavy-handed. If you have too many seedlings in a bed or pot, they won't produce as well. In order to avoid crowding, we have to thin the seedlings out. Remember that the first leaves that appear after seeding are called the seed leaves or cotyledons. The second set of leaves are the true leaves, and will look very different from the seed leaves. Wait for the true leaves before dividing or transplanting. Seed leaves appear quickly and manufacture food from sunlight–photosynthesis. If the plant is damaged at this stage, it won't come back. Once they get the second set of leaves, there is a stronger root system and they can come back. Think about all those oak seedlings we all have in our yards right now. If you can mow them or weed-eat them as soon as they appear, they won't come back. If you allow them to get several sets of leaves, mowing them simply slows them down and they put on more leaves. When seeding squash or cucumbers, you can have 2 to 3 seedlings per mound but more than that will compete for the space.

Female squash flower developing

Garlic harvest

Onion blooms

HARVEST

HARVEST OF COOL-SEASON vegetables is in full swing. We should have ample harvests of lettuce, greens, onions, broccoli and spinach. If you do have cool-season crops in the garden, you may see some of them bolting, or going to seed. This simply tells you that their growing season is over and you need to use them, or lose them. Once your onion plants form a flower stalk, their season is over, and you will see no increase in bulb size. Many folks think they can cut these bloom stalks off and reverse the process, but that isn't so. Harvest and use any cool-season vegetable when you see a bloom stalk forming. As you harvest plants, replant the space with more vegetables. If you planted early warm-season crops, you will soon get squash, green beans and peppers.

Strawberry season is still going strong. Avoid fertilization of your strawberry beds until after you harvest. If you fertilize too early it can result in extra foliage, which can lead to more fruit rot. More foliage means more shading of the fruit and cuts down on air circulation. Watch out for slugs, which like the berries as much as we do. Mulching can help keep the fruit cleaner, but it also tends to be a haven for slugs. Once your season is over, renovate the beds. This is something you need to do every year or your beds become a tangled mess of strawberry plants. Renovating will cut down on production. Thin the beds back to the original plant spacing, then fertilize.

Plant of the Month

Potato

Solanum tuberosum

POTATOES HAVE A LONG HISTORY and are easy to grow in the garden. The potato, *Solanum tuberosum,* is the world's fourth largest food crop, following rice, wheat and maize. The Incan in Peru grew potatoes around 8,000 BC to 5,000 B.C. Sir Walter Raleigh introduced potatoes to Ireland in 1589 where it became a staple crop. When the potato blight swept through Europe in the 1840s, it wiped out the potato crop, leading to widespread famine in Ireland. Over the course of the famine, almost 1 million people died from starvation or disease and another 1 million people left Ireland, mostly for Canada and the United States.

Potatoes are typically planted from a small potato with eyes called a seed potato. Most garden centers sell them from February through April. There are many potato varieties with reds, yellows, and blue forms. They can be planted in late winter for an early summer harvest, or planted in late summer for a fall harvest, but seed potatoes can be hard to find for fall plantings. They can be planted 3 to 5 inches deep and 18 to 24 inches apart in well-drained soil in full sun. Rotate where you plant potatoes each year to cut back on disease issues.

Potatoes require good soil moisture when the foliage is actively growing. An uneven water supply can cause knobs to form on the potatoes or cracks to appear. As the vines begin to yellow at the end of the season, let them dry out a bit. If they are too wet, it can lead to rotting of the potatoes. If you plan to eat the potatoes quickly, you can harvest as the vines die back, but if you have planted a lot and want to store potatoes, wait two weeks after the vines die back to harvest. Small new potatoes can be harvested when they are large enough to eat, but must be used fairly quickly after harvest.

The main insect problem for potatoes is the Colorado potato beetle. This hard-shelled, yellow-with-black-stripe beetle can wreak havoc on the plants. The adults lay eggs on the plants and the pinkish larvae can defoliate a plant quite quickly. While there are a lot of diseases associated with potatoes, we don't usually have too many in the home garden. A scaly appearance on the outer skin of the potato, called scab, is usually associated with high-pH soil. Avoid using lime around potato plants. While this condition doesn't look too appetizing, it doesn't affect the quality of the inside of the potato.

Q & A

Q. I have planted seeds of broccoli, cauliflower and Brussels sprouts this spring and have not had much luck with the plants maturing and growing. Once the temperatures have warmed up, they really did not grow much. What can I do next year to have a better crop of these vegetables?

A. All of the vegetables you mentioned are in the cole crop family and need to be planted from transplants, not seeds. Most home gardeners have good success with broccoli, but cauliflower and Brussels sprouts are not the easiest vegetables to grow in the home garden, especially as a spring crop. You are correct that these plants don't do well when the temperatures start to heat up. Fall planting can give you better results, but even then, we often don't get a large number of fruits on Brussels sprouts. One thing that can help on your Brussels sprouts is to pinch or remove the growing point of the plant now. This may help in the development of some sprouts even this late. Huge fluctuations in temperature can cause an interruption in the growth of the cauliflower and Brussels sprouts which can abort the development of the edible portion. All of these plants are heavy feeders, so I hope you kept up with fertilization. Start interplanting with your summer squash now and give the cole crops until the first of June and see what happens.

Q. We plant corn in our garden every year, but the worms get it before we do. How can we keep the worms out? They just ruin all of our corn every year.

A. Corn earworms are destructive. When you see the silks beginning to form, you need to take action. You can sprinkle a little sevin dust on the silks every few days, or do what I think is easier (and safer for our bees): put a drop or two of mineral oil right on the silk once a week until the silks turn brown. The oil acts as a physical barrier and keeps the worms out. Don't get heavy handed and pour a bunch of oil in, or it can affect kernel set. Typically there is only one earworm per ear of corn since these caterpillars are cannibalistic, and eat each other as well as the corn. Occasionally you will have two–one on each side–they just don't know the other one is there!

Q. I moved to Van Buren 366 days ago. I started tilling my garden in January due to the unusually mild temperatures. I was able to start planting potatoes in March and in the first week of April I planted 70

tomato plants, 56 pepper, 16 yellow squash, 4 zucchini and the list goes on. Everything was looking great until yesterday. We were hit with a hail storm, the likes of which I had never experienced. My 40 feet by 75 feet garden looks like a weed eater came through and cut some in half and others the stem may be all that is left. Will the plants possibly survive? Can I do anything to try and save what is left? My thoughts were to wait a week to 10 days and see what plants look like. If they don't make it I will replace them.

A. Hail can wreak havoc, and some plants will rebound, while others won't. The key is to clean up as much as you can. Broken or jagged branches or stems can be a target for diseases. Once you have it clean, see what continues to grow, and what doesn't. Replanting some things will be inevitable, but some plants are more resilient than others. We missed a late freeze, and then you got hail. Gardening isn't for sissies!

Q. Each year I have tiny black pests on the leaves of vegetables in my garden. They cause damage to my plants and are difficult and expensive to try to control. They are so tiny, they are almost invisible to the naked eye. You almost need a magnifying glass. I can only see them if I cut off some leaves and shake the leaves on a piece of white paper. Then I can see the tiny black dots move around. What are they and how do I control them?

A. The most common insect in the garden is aphids. They can be black, red, green or yellow. They are small and tend to congregate near new growth or in the joints of leaves. Flea beetles are also small, but tend to jump with vigor when disturbed. Spider mites are really tiny but tend to be reddish in color. If aphids are the culprit, they can be controlled with a strong spray of water, insecticidal soap or Malathion. Be sure to follow label directions as to timing and harvesting. For a definitive diagnosis of the insect, take some into your local county extension office.

Q. What is the safest way to control weeds and grass growing in a vegetable garden? The garden is approximately 30 feet by 40 feet, therefore, not easy to apply mulch. We till, but weeds and grass will return.

A. The Santa Claus method–hoe, hoe, hoe–is actually the safest and most effective way to control weeds in the vegetable garden. While there are some herbicides that are labeled for gardens, they are usually not recommended for all vegetables, and the waiting period may be too long for you to use. Hoeing is actually preferable to the tiller. Tilling is easier, but actually brings up more weed seeds from down below, which leads to more weeds. Cutting the weeds off at the surface and then mulching is the best thing you can do for your garden. There are lots of mulch options. Spread down newspaper or shred your junk mail and lay that down. It doesn't have to be as aesthetically pleasing in the vegetable garden as it does in ornamental beds. Mulching that large of a garden may seem like a lot of work on the front end, but the amount of weeds it will cut down will make it worth the effort.

Q & A

Q. Our vegetable garden consists of 2 grape-type tomato plants that are having a problem you can hopefully resolve. Something is eating a perfectly round hole about a quarter inch deep and the same size in diameter but nothing is ever visible on them. I have sprayed once with an insecticide to no avail. Obviously even the bugs and worms don't respect the elderly!

A. Grape tomatoes don't have a lot to feed on, so any feeding is doing real damage! Tomato fruit worms can make very defined holes, but you usually find the worm and/or their droppings. Check the stems and leaves around the plants as well. Could birds be coming in to have a taste? Try using bird netting around your plants to discourage them, and see if new damage continues. If it is a caterpillar, then BT or Dipel can work, but it will take a week or so to work. Go out in the evening and see if you can spot anything working on them.

Q. I live in northwest Arkansas and we have some small cedar trees at the edge of our lawn that has some orange (fungus?) looking things growing out of gray nuts. They look like a bunch of tentacles and are mushy. Are these harmful to the cedars?

A. What you are seeing with the bright orange tentacles is the fruiting body of cedar/apple rust on your cedar tree. This disease has two hosts: Eastern red cedar and apples/crabapples. The disease first starts on the cedar. During periods of rain in the spring the galls quickly grow orange, gelatinous tentacles that produce spores that blow to the developing fruit and leaves on nearby apple and crabapple trees. Symptoms will appear on apple foliage as small round orange spots, which then yellow. Heavy infestations can cause the apple trees to shed foliage and lightly deform the fruit, but the disease is not deadly to either plant. If you desire clean fruit, fruit sprays are needed in early spring. They are only effective during the time the spores are active in early spring, and once you see symptoms, sprays are no longer effective. If you don't grow apple trees, you can ignore them or simply enjoy their odd appearance. Refer to this online fact sheet: www.uaex.edu/publications/PDF/FSA-7538.pdf.

Q. All of a sudden I've been reading articles in magazines and newspapers about growing blueberry bushes in a pot for fruit in summer, colorful foliage in fall. Can you recommend a good bush to thrive in central Arkansas?

A. Almost any edible vegetable or fruit can be grown in containers, and blueberries are no exception. I would definitely opt for the largest container you can manage to make watering easier. Blueberries are not drought tolerant. They like a rich soil with plenty of organic matter, at least 6 hours of sunlight and even moisture. Many parts of central Arkanas are known for rocky soil, so raised beds or containers would make planting easier. You can grow either the southern high-bush varieties: Legacy, Summit or Ozarkblue; or the Rabbiteye varieties: Climax, Premier, Brightwell or Tifblue. Remember you need at least two varieties to grow fruit. They are beautiful plants with pretty white flowers in the spring, tasty and showy blueberries and outstanding fall color.

Q. I planted garlic for the first time this year. I planted it in October, and it has done great all winter and still looks great. My question is when do I harvest it? The leaves are full and grassy-like and dark green, but I don't know if I should pull it and eat it now, or wait for it to bloom like I see my onions doing.

A. For fall-planted garlic, you normally harvest the garlic when the leaves begin to die back, which will occur in late June or July. This means the garlic is mature and will store well after harvest. If you have planted quite a few, you can harvest a few plants and use them as green garlic. If you are growing hardneck cultivars and they send up a flower stalk, you can also harvest those and use them like you would green onions. If you have planted more than you can use quickly, store them like you would dry onions in a cool dry area with good air circulation. You can also braid the tops together and hang in your kitchen and take a bulb as needed.

Q. I have a problem of big radish leaves and no radish under the ground. What is my problem?

A. A couple of things can cause this: too much nitrogen fertilizer, which puts all the energy to foliage, or heavy soil. Add compost or a little sand into the soil at planting to give them a light, airy soil to grow in, and use a well-balanced fertilizer at planting and again 6 to 8 weeks later. Also, make sure you have at least 6 to 8 hours of sunlight a day; otherwise, they may not be getting enough energy to produce a radish.

Q. I have sprouted some pecans. When these plants are mature enough, will they produce fruit that is the same as the one the plants were grown from?

A. Pecans cross-pollinate to set nuts. That means the resulting pecans, if planted, will have genetic characteristics of both parents. They may be similar to what you had to begin with, or totally different–you won't know until they begin to bear nuts in 7 to 10 years. However, you can graft cuttings from the tree where you harvested the pecans onto the seedlings next year and you will be guaranteed the same quality nuts–provided insects or diseases don't alter that, or you can spray during the growing season.

JUNE

EVEN IF YOUR VEGETABLE garden got off to a slow start, they should be kicking in now. Don't worry if you haven't planted a garden yet, there is still time to plant warm-season vegetables, and now is a great time to plant pumpkins and gourds for a fall harvest. You can also plant tomatoes, eggplants and peppers, along with okra and summer peas. Be sure to water, mulch and fertilize. Make sure all plants in the garden are mulched; this reduces weeds, prevents soil from splashing onto the stems and fruit and moderates soil temperature and moisture levels. Mulching can really make a difference in your maintenance routine. Gardens in the sun will dry out faster, heat up more and are usually more weed infested–especially with Bermuda grass.

Blueberry bloom

Make sure your gardens are in good shape now before the real heat of summer hits. If you have plants in containers, remember the larger the pot, the easier they are to maintain.

Sale of edible plants has increased dramatically in recent years. Many nurseries will see fruit trees flying off the shelves. While peaches are often on the top of home gardeners' lists, they are the hardest for a homeowner to maintain. Diseases are really a problem with peaches, so regular spray schedules are a must. Easier fruits for home gardeners to maintain include figs, Oriental persimmons, pears and even apples. Small fruits can actually serve as ornamentals. Blueberries are beautiful in bloom, in fruit and have an outstanding fall color. Strawberries would make a great groundcover and muscadines can cover an arbor in no time.

Peaches

HARVEST

Okra bloom

VEGETABLE GARDENS ARE POPPING. The final harvest season is upon us for the cool-season vegetables and we are beginning to harvest our warm-season crops. As your cool-season vegetables are harvested, replant with heat lovers. You want to utilize as much space in the garden as possible. Okra, southern peas and winter squash will all thrive now. If you want pumpkins and gourds in time for Halloween, plant between June 15 and July 15. Water and mulch these plants to help get them established. The temperatures are warming up, humidity is increasing and so are your chances for insects and diseases. Pay attention to your garden on a regular basis. The earlier you can catch a problem and handle it, the less likely it will be to destroy the garden.

If you have planted both a cool-season and a warm-season vegetable, you are now reaping the benefits of your planting. We are getting a bountiful harvest of lettuce, broccoli, cabbage, onions and new potatoes. Swiss chard, kale and other greens are also still producing. Some early squash and green beans are also available and it won't be long before we harvest the first tomato! Harvest your garden regularly to get the most from your plants.

As temperatures heat up, rainfall also tends to become spottier, so June is the time to start monitoring the water needs. Water is still the most vital ingredient for success in any garden, but pay attention to fertilizer needs and monitor for diseases and insects. Insects and diseases seem to be at a premium almost every year. Make sure that you dump out any standing water that is in your yard. Remove the saucers from under your flowerpots, and check out birdbaths and kids toys that can hold water. If you have regular water in the yard, you can get mosquito dunks or granules from your local nursery or hardware store. These are put in the water to keep mosquitoes from breeding.

The first report of blossom end rot is on the horizon. We typically get our first calls on this in early June,

Strawberries

and often right after a heavy downpour. Blossom end rot starts as a water-soaked spot on the bottom of the tomato, which quickly turns black. While it looks like an awful disease, it is a physiological disorder–a calcium deficiency–and is often associated with fluctuations in soil moisture levels. Nothing will reverse the damage on the affected fruit, but you can help prevent the problem by mulching your plants and maintaining an even moisture level. Sprays of calcium chloride commonly sold as Stop Rot or Rot Stop can help put calcium back in the plants. Water your garden early in the day to allow moisture to enter the soil with the least amount of evaporation, and to help the plants dry before nightfall. Calcium levels are also a factor–make sure your soil pH is high enough. A soil test can determine this, but a light application of lime to the planting soil can also help.

If you have established strawberries, thin out your plantings as soon as possible after harvest. Remove the mulch and thin plants to 6 to 8 inches apart. The remaining plants will produce new runner plants to fill back in for the next season. Fertilize to encourage vigorous top growth. Water and mulch your strawberry plants as needed. If you don't thin annually, you will end up with a matted row of plants, which will not be as productive.

Plant of the Month

Tomatoes

Solanum Lycopersicum

IT'S THAT MOMENT WE DREAM about all winter, as we muddle through with mere substitutes.

There is nothing like that first bite of a home grown, juicy tomato. Few vegetables–or is that fruits?–bring about more opinions than tomatoes. They are the number one vegetable planted in home gardens and it seems everyone has their favorite variety. Whether it is the original Arkansas pink tomato–the Bradley–or the Arkansas Traveler, the Better Boy, Roma, Sweet 100, Yellow Pear or the giant Beefsteak, they are truly good eating and can be easily grown in the home garden from transplants.

There are hundreds of varieties of tomatoes on the market from new cultivars with disease resistance to the old-fashioned heirloom varieties. It is important for disease control that you rotate your tomatoes, not planting in the same spot each year. There are numerous diseases of tomatoes and they often hit earlier and earlier each year if planted in the same spot. Newer varieties have letters following their names. VFNT stand for resistance to Verticillium wilt, fusarium wilt, nematodes and tobacco mosaic virus. But even resistant varieties can get diseases if you plant in the same soil year after year.

There are two basic types of tomato plants–determinate and indeterminate–often referred to as bush or tall-growing plants. Determinate plants are self-topping, typically form a stronger main stem and have a bushier growth. The top buds set fruits, thus stopping the continuation of growth. They are often sold as patio tomatoes. Indeterminate tomatoes continue to grow all season, unless you top them. Plants can grow to 12 to 15 feet or more and require staking for support. As long as they are healthy, they will continue to produce until a freeze in the fall.

Regardless of which type you are growing, they need a minimum of 6 to 8 hours of sun and even moisture. They have complete flowers with both male and female parts together, so they don't need bees to pollinate them. Regular fertilization will help with production. Normally, we broadcast a complete fertilizer at planting and then side-dress every 3 to 4 weeks while the plants are producing. Staking the plants is necessary for indeterminate varieties, but helpful even with the patio varieties giving the plants more stability while they are fruiting.

So whether you like red, orange, yellow or even black-fruited varieties, there is a tomato plant to satisfy all gardeners. If you have a surplus, you can always make salsa, tomato sauce or share with friends. If you haven't planted, there is still plenty of time, and if you planted early, you aren't that far from your first harvest.

Q & A

Q. I have a large planting of Kentucky Wonder pole beans that have huge vines and absolutely no flowers or beans. They get plenty of sunlight. What can I do to encourage flowers–should I use more fertilizer or water more? I enriched the soil well with compost at planting, and have fertilized twice. All of my other plants are doing great.

A. You have probably created too rich an environment for your beans. They are so busy growing they simply haven't slowed down enough to set fruit. No more fertilization is needed, or you will make the problem worse–especially with nitrogen. Try topping the vines back, and cutting back on your watering. What you want to do is stress them so they will stop growing and start producing. Beans are low nitrogen users and if over-fertilized will not produce well.

Q. My husband and I have a great vegetable garden. We have, for the last few years, grown "burpless" cucumbers that are wonderful. Toward the end of last year we realized that they are bitter. What is going on with this? Are we doing something? Could it be the weather?

A. It most definitely can be the weather. Cucumbers contain a bitter compound called cucurbitacin, which can be present in the fruit as well as the foliage. If the plant is stressed, from dry conditions, high heat or low nutrition, it can cause bitterness. Try mulching your plants, moderating soil moisture and hopefully you can control the bitterness. The burpless varieties are supposed to have less bitterness, but they can get stressed, too.

Q. I have 14 eggplants and they were all planted at the same time. They are now fairly large and have bushed out, but only two of the plants have had any blooms—one bloom each, and right now I have two beautiful little eggplants. There are no other blooms in sight. Flea beetles and aphids were a real problem early on, but I have killed all of those and now leaf hoppers are attacking. Many of the older leaves have large holes, like a caterpillar or slug has attacked, but I have seen neither, nor the silvery lines from slugs. I love eggplants, and this is the first year I have attempted to grow them. To have such big plants and no blooms is disappointing. As of now, I have used no fertilizer or manure. The rest of my garden has had the same conditions, but seems to be faring well. I have peppers, tomatoes, squash, cucumbers, onions, beans, watermelon and cantaloupe. Please help!

A. I think you should be patient. Eggplants like heat, and unlike other vegetables don't slow down when the temperatures heat up so there is still plenty of time to harvest huge quantities of them this season. Water when dry, and fertilize. You could top-dress with some well-rotted manure, and use a complete fertilizer. Mulch the plants to conserve moisture. Do monitor for pest problems, and control as needed. Flea beetles are a common problem with eggplants and can leave the plants looking like they were shot through with tiny holes.

Q. A friend gave me some gourd seeds for birds' nests. I planted them and they're a few feet tall now and probably need fertilizer. What type should I use and how often should I apply it? Is this vine an annual or will it come back on its own next year? How do I treat them to make birds' nests?

A. I assume you are referring to birdhouse gourds, the ones that grow 10- to 12-inches long and taper at the one end to hang. They should have been fertilized at planting with a complete fertilizer (something with all three numbers like 10-10-10 and again 6 to 8 weeks into the growing season. Too much nitrogen will encourage rapid vine growth and can deter fruit set. To get the prettiest shape, you may want to grow them on a trellis so the gourds will hang down straight. The fruits should mature in the fall, and the outer shell will become hard. When harvesting, be sure to leave an inch or two of stem attached. Cure the gourds for a few days after harvesting in the shade. Wash dirty fruits and rinse in a weak bleach solution before final drying. Hang them on wires until completely dry in a warm, dry area. Then make them into a birdhouse. They are an annual vine, so save some seeds if you wish to replant next season.

Q. I am new to gardening and wanted to grow cucumbers to make my own pickles, but instead of straight cucumbers, they are crooked and misshapen. Will they develop into normal cucumbers?

A. The crooked cucumbers will not straighten up over time, but you can still eat them. Misshapen cucumbers result from poor pollination or low fertility. Side-dressing plants with a complete fertilizer may help later cucumbers develop normally and try to encourage bees to your garden.

Q. Please tell me why one of my tomato plants has a black spot on the bottom of each tomato. I have six tomato plants in large pots on my patio. All plants are doing great and look beautiful except this one.

A. It sounds like the one plant is suffering from blossom end rot. This problem occurs more commonly on some varieties than others. It is a calcium deficiency that is made worse when we have major fluctuations of water–and if a plant is vigorously growing. The calcium gets pulled from the bottom end of the tomato and you are left with a water-soaked area, which then rots or turns black. Mulching (even in pots) can help to moderate moisture. Adding a little lime into the soil at planting can also help, or you can lightly work it into the soil in the pot.

Q & A

Q. I have planted some tomatoes in pots and all seem to be okay except one whose leaves are curling. It does not seem to have as deep green color to the leaves. What could be the problem? Also what causes the blossom end to rot and what can be done for that?

A. Leaf roll (curling of the leaflets) is a physiological condition that occurs most commonly when plants are trained and pruned. Any type of stress can cause leaf roll. It usually does not affect fruiting or quality, and it is not a disease. Leaf roll is a common genetic trait in some varieties, but it is typically not associated with a difference in leaf color. Monitor these plants, make sure you are watering enough, but don't drown them either. Use a water-soluble fertilizer and see if that helps with the color. Blossom end rot is a calcium deficiency that is usually brought about with huge fluctuations in moisture levels–we often see it when we go through a dry spell and then have a downpour of rain. Even though your plants are in containers, mulch the soil to aid in keeping the moisture levels more constant.

Q. I am growing three tomato plants in containers on my deck. One of my tomato plant's leaves have a yellow tint around their edges. The leaves affected are on the northwest side of the bush. The bush is either a Bush Early Girl or a Health Kick. They may not be getting enough sunshine. Do you think that is the problem?

A. Growing tomatoes in pots gives you a clean slate every season, because you can start with fresh soil. Therefore, diseases are at a minimum. I doubt lack of sun on one side of the bush would cause yellowing. If no spots are involved, the problem could be nutritional in nature. Fertility in plants grown in containers becomes more of an issue, since you are watering more frequently which leaches the nutrients out. Make sure your plants are getting at least 6 to 8 hours of sunlight a day. Fertilize with a water soluble fertilizer every 10 days to two weeks. Monitor the plants and see what happens.

Q. My tomatoes have developed a yellow blight on the bottom leaves, causing the leaves to slowly die. The disease works to the top of the plant and finally kills the plant. I have had the same problem for the last couple of years. This year I am using a fungicide and am spraying twice a week. I wonder if I am using the right fungicide or should I use something else? I am also wondering if the blight is in the soil.

A. Tomato plants suffer from a variety of soil-borne diseases and several start with yellowing of leaves from the bottom and work their way up. Two of the most common are septoria leaf spot and early blight. Early blight appears as spots on leaves, stems and fruit. Leaf spots start as small, dark brown areas, sometimes with a yellow border. Leaf spots grow rapidly under favorable conditions, forming lighter brown bands with a dark center. Stem spots have even more noticeable rings than leaf spots and may cause plant death if the stem is girdled. Another common disease that can be controlled is septoria leaf spot. Spots on lower leaves usually show up as the first tomatoes start setting and may also form on stems and branches. Spots are round, and smaller than the early blight–about an eighth of an inch across, with dark-brown borders and light-gray centers. Young spots may be surrounded by a yellow halo as well. The disease progresses up the plant from the older to younger leaves, spread by splashing rain or overhead irrigation. Fruit infection is rare. Both diseases can be controlled with a product containing chlorothalonil, of which there are numerous trade names including Bravo, Daconil and Ortho's Garden Disease Control. The key is not to wait to see the disease and start playing catch-up with fungicides. It is much easier to prevent than cure the disease. Rotate your plants in the garden–don't plant tomatoes back in the same soil for at least 3 years. If you get the disease annually, start spraying when you plant and continue throughout the season. Since you can still harvest tomatoes with both of these diseases, you could grow the plants with proper cultural conditions–water, sunlight, mulch and fertility and harvest what you can until the plants play out. Then replant in a new location mid-summer to have tomatoes for a fall harvest.

Q. My tomatoes are blooming but are not making tomatoes. Is there anything I can do?

A. Be patient. Tomatoes can be finicky, not setting fruit when the nights are too cool or too hot, nor when the days are rainy or over 90 degrees. You can lightly shake the plants to help set the pollen, but with time fruits should begin to form.

JULY

Fennel bloom

Tomato

Sage

THE HEAT IS ON! From now until the end of summer, temperatures and humidity only seem to get worse, so water is the most important factor in your garden. To keep a garden growing, it is important that you monitor your rainfall and water needs. Water is always the most important factor for success. Rainfall tends to be spotty at best, so you really can't rely on the weatherman to know how much rain your yard gets. Make sure your garden has a rain gauge so you know what is happening in your yard.

Correct watering is important to plant health. Try not to water too long before the sun is up and finish well before the sun sets. Keeping water on the foliage and fruits too long can lead to disease problems. While it is more efficient to water early in the day, if you have to hand-water or drag hoses and you aren't home in the mornings, watering when you have the time is important. Mid-day watering is not as efficient because we tend to lose more water to evaporation, but the key is getting water to the plants. Giving your plants time to dry before sunset will also be healthier for the plants. Drip irrigation that can keep the moisture on the ground and off the plants is worth looking into for many gardeners.

Timing is also important. How long should you water? The goal is to give our plants an inch or two of water per week. But there are many variables to consider: type of soil, type of plants and spacing, amount of sunlight and slope of your yard. You want the water to be able to penetrate down in the soil, not run off down the street. Deep, infrequent watering is better than daily showers. Container plants in full sun need daily water when it is hot.

Weakened plants are more susceptible to diseases and insects. As the season progresses, so do problems with diseases and insects. Aphids, white flies and spider mites are all poor swimmers and thrive in dry conditions. Using a spray from the garden hose can knock them down, but pay attention and try to catch them when they get started. There are numerous insecticides on the market that can work. As with any pest problem, the sooner you catch them, the easier they are to control. Be careful with applying any pesticide when plants are stressed by hot, dry conditions. Make sure the plants have ample moisture in them before spraying. Other insects that are becoming a problem include grasshoppers. They can ravage a plant in a short amount of time, so move quickly when you see problems. Monitor your plants, and if you have problems and aren't sure what they are, take a good sample to your local county extension office. If they can't diagnose it, they can send it on to the disease diagnostic lab for diagnosis. Taking samples in on a Monday or Tuesday is a good idea when temperatures are so hot. They want the samples arriving in good shape, not sitting in a post office all weekend.

Some tomatoes struggle across the state. Many of the diseases are soil-borne. Heavy rains or frequent overhead irrigation cause the soil to get splashed up on the stems, which can help to spread these diseases. Some of the plants are too far gone to salvage, but you should continue to harvest as tomatoes ripen. Consider planting new plants in a different section of the garden to give you a later harvest. Rotation of crops–not planting in the same spot for three years–can lessen your chances of diseases hitting quite so quickly. Also be on the lookout for tomato hornworms. They camouflage themselves quite nicely but can quickly decimate a tomato plant.

HARVEST

If you are growing tomatoes–the number one vegetable in the home garden–don't be alarmed if your plants quit setting fruit in the hottest days of summer. Many varieties won't set fruit if the daytime temperatures exceed 95 degrees and the nighttime temperatures stay above 75. Keep the plants watered and mulched, and they should rebound and begin to set fruit once the temperatures settle down. If the plants are strong and viable, they can continue to bear tomatoes through frost. If blights have taken their toll, consider starting some new plants from the suckers of your existing plants, or buying new plants.

Gardens that have been watered and maintained are producing a bountiful harvest. Harvest vegetables early in the day for best flavor. Remember that peppers are heavy feeders and need plenty of nutrition to keep producing. Use caution when applying fertilizer or pesticides when the weather is hot and dry. Make sure there is ample moisture in the ground and in the plants before fertilizing. Avoid using many pesticides, and if you have to spray, do so very early in the day after you have irrigated.

If you are going on vacation, don't just abandon your vegetable garden. Find a friend to come check on the garden, pick vegetables when they are ripe, water and scout for problems. Leaving your vegetables on the plants long after they are ripe can slow down production, but can also lead to rotted fruits which will attract insects and animals to the garden. If you are finished harvesting, practice good sanitation and remove the spent plants. You can replant with southern peas, okra and even pepper and tomato plants. Check your local garden center and you will be amazed what is still available. In a month we start planting the fall garden.

Blackberries and raspberries are becoming more common in the home garden. These plants need annual care after harvest. The canes that bear fruit this year need to be pruned out at the soil line following harvest. The canes will die back on their own, but removing them will keep the plants healthy and the garden clean. The new canes that are growing this season will bear fruit next summer. Keep the plants pruned to a manageable height to make picking easier next year, mulch the beds and watch for runners. Blackberries in particular are notorious for sending out new plants far beyond where you want them.

July is a good month for fresh fruit. There are still blackberries in July and peaches are ripening, along with later blueberries and the early apples. Figs will be in season soon and some early grapes are hitting the market as well. If you don't grow your own, don't forget about the wonderful network of farmers markets across the state. Today's farmers markets are not just about vegetables, they're also great sources for fresh flower bouquets, locally grown meat, jams, jellies and breads. Some even offer locally made craft items. Not only do you have access to fresh, locally grown produce, you get to mingle with neighbors and friends while shopping. For many, the farmers market is a highlight of their week.

Plant of the Month

OKRA

Abelmoschus Esculentus

OKRA IS A TRUE SOUTHERN VEGETABLE belonging to the Mallow family, which includes cotton and hibiscus. The Latin name is *Hibiscus esculentus,* and if you have ever seen an okra bloom, you will notice the similarity to hibiscus. Okra likes warm, well-drained soils, so it is not usually planted until May. It thrives in the heat of an Arkansas summer and is a plant that can grow 6 feet or more in height. This is a plant we typically grow from seed. Broadcast a complete fertilizer at seeding and again when the plants are about 6 to 8 inches tall, then again in 3 to 4 weeks. Don't overdo it with too much nitrogen or you can get huge plants with limited production.

Okra plants begin to flower within a month and a half from seeding. Harvest the immature seedpods when they are between 2 to 4 inches in length. People have different preferences to the size of okra, but if left too long, the pods get tough and woody. If you don't harvest frequently–every few days during production–you will also limit the amount of new pods produced. It is best to use scissors or pruning shears to harvest, as the pods are firmly attached and the small spines on the fruits and stems can irritate some people's skin.

Okra plants continue to produce until frost, as long as pods are removed or harvested regularly. Most pods are ready for harvesting 4 to 6 days after the bloom opens. The immature pods can be used in soups and stew, or served fried, boiled and pickled.

Clemson Spineless is the most common variety of okra, but Lee and Jade were developed by the University of Arkansas System's Division of Agriculture. A red-podded form called Red Burgundy can be quite showy in the garden and will have green pods once cooked.

Q & A

Q. Is it possible to grow bell peppers as large as those found in the grocery store? My wife keeps picking them well before they get huge, and I want the big ones.

A. While it is possible to grow large bell peppers in a home garden, it isn't easy. Peppers need high nutrition and plenty of water. Fertilize them regularly throughout the growing season. Once your peppers begin turning a dull color or changing from bright green to red, growth has stopped and you may as well pick them, unless you want red peppers. But there is hope: Peppers can produce up until frost, so keep up with their care. There is also some varietal difference as to eventual mature size.

Q. Thanks for the information on how to keep the worms from sweet corn. Now, please advise me how to keep the squirrels away.

A. If only there was a solution for squirrels that was as effective as the one for corn earworms! Fencing, scare devices–a big dog–are options, but squirrels are tenacious. Some gardeners trap the squirrels with have-a-heart traps, but you would need a lot of traps in my neighborhood. Others have tried feeding the squirrels in an area away from the garden, but then you end up inviting more squirrels to your yard, and they may look at your corn as just extra food. Try a variety of approaches, and good luck!

Q. Why am I not getting any squash? I keep getting these gorgeous male blossoms, but the lower female blossoms appear to be rotting off the stems. Am I watering too much or perhaps not enough? I have seen and killed several squash bugs and/or stink bugs, but I have not seen them for a while. In the meantime, I continue to see these healthy-looking plants with new beautiful blossoms, but no squash or zucchini.

A. You aren't alone. Summer squash seems to be much more affected by heat than other members of the cucurbits. Even those with beehives in their backyard are having an issue. For some, a lack of pollinators can affect the fruit set. Squash has separate male and female flowers, and to get squash something needs to transfer pollen from the male bloom to the female bloom. If you don't have bees, you can do it yourself with a paint brush or Q-tip. Squash flowers won't open for long on hot days, so it lessens the opportunity for pollination. If your female flowers aren't open long, there is little chance of fruit set. I would not blame it on a damaging insect or lack of bees, but I would blame it on the weather. Maybe you should pull up the squash and use that space for okra and more peppers, which can take the heat.

Q. What is the reason and solution for blooms falling from tomato plants? The flowers can't seem to stay long enough for fruit to appear. What do I do?

A. Tomato blossoms fail to set fruit when the nighttime temperature stays above 75 degrees, and/or when the daytime temperature exceeds 95 degrees. It's the reason we often have no tomatoes during a killer summer. There isn't much you can do about it, but keep the plants healthy and happy until the weather cools off and they begin to bear again.

Q. My tomatoes have died because of what I think is a blight. If this is in the soil of my garden, is there any way I could sterilize the soil so I could plant some late tomatoes and have some this fall? Is there some fungicide I could use that would prevent it?

A. There are numerous diseases that plague tomatoes. Early blight, septoria leaf spot and late blight cause the "firing" up of the lower leaves. It usually takes the plant by the end of the season, but you usually have had a good harvest by then. Weekly fungicide sprays can help to prevent it. If your plants out-and-out died already, you may have one of the more serious vascular wilts. These soil-borne diseases can kill a plant within a few days' time once they hit. Soil sterilization can be done via the sun, called soil solarization. Chemical products are no longer available to the home gardener. To solarize your soil, till it thoroughly, wet it completely, then cover it with clear plastic, making firm contact between soil and plastic. Leave it covered for 6 weeks. Then you can replant. You could have a good crop of fall tomatoes. You could also get them growing in large containers. Tomatoes can be container-grown all season, just keep up with the watering

Q. My grandmother is having a problem with her tomatoes. It has been happening the last several years. Her tomato plants look wonderful one day, wilt the next and die the day after. She has tried several varieties, and they all have this same problem.

A. From the quick death of the plants, my guess would be bacterial wilt or possibly one of the vascular wilts, either fusarium or verticillium wilt. All of these tomato diseases are soil-borne and there is no spray program that will work to prevent them. Cut the lower or main stem and look inside at the vascular tissue. Fusarium wilt causes a dark brown discoloration within the vascular tissue. Fusarium crown rot causes a rot or canker at the base of the stem and possibly a root rot. Bacterial wilt typically causes rapid wilting and death of plants without yellowing or spotting of leaves. Brown discoloration and decay are evident inside the stems of infected plants. The disease is easily diagnosed by suspending a clean, cut section of diseased stem in clear water. A white milky stream of bacterial cells will start to flow out from infected stems into the water after a few minutes. Look for varieties labeled with a VF which are resistant to verticillium and fusarium wilt. Do not plant tomatoes, potatoes or eggplant in the affected area for two or three years. No fungicides are labeled for control of any of these problems. If you want an accurate diagnosis of the problem, take one of the dying plants into your local extension office. Take the lower crown and roots. They can send it to the disease diagnostic lab for diagnosis. Sanitation is important, and if the problem is in a

Q & A

small section of the garden you can solarize the soil now by removing the diseased plants, wetting the soil thoroughly and covering with clear plastic. Leave it covered for 6 to 8 weeks, and the heat may kill many of the disease organisms.

Q. Our tomato plants are pathetic. They are planted in good soil, and I am fertilizing with Miracle Grow, but not doing it too often. I have not used any insecticides. The plant blooms appear and then fall off after a few days. Do we need bees? I have not seen a single one in Garland County, although they must be somewhere!

A. Tomato plants produce a complete flower, which means they have the male and female parts together in the same bloom. Wind movement is usually enough to set the fruit, so bees are not needed for pollination. Keep in mind that the flowers are only viable for a short period of time, and if the temperatures are hot–above 90 to 95 degrees, during the day and above 70 to 75 degrees at night–tomatoes won't set fruit. Keep the plants healthy and happy and they should set fruit once the weather straightens out. As long as they are blooming, they are getting enough sunlight.

Q. Our tomato plants started to die, and we pulled one up and found what looked like little white rocks on the roots. You could crush them with your finger. The tomatoes don't taste as good as they did last year.

A. If you still have the plant handy, take a closer look. Were there small, mustard-seed-like growths at the soil line or at the crown of the plant? Southern stem blight can kill a plant. Usually you will see some small white mustard seed like growths at the base. They will turn brown in time, but usually the plant is on its way out at that point. When you pulled the plants up, had the root system spread out or were the roots stunted and the ends of the roots had the small growths? This could be a root knot nematode. Here is an excellent publication the extention has on tomatoes with color images to help you pinpoint the problem: www.uaex.edu/publications/pdf/FSA-7568.pdf. You can also take a sample of a damaged plant in to your local extension office for further diagnosis.

Q. A couple of years ago, I was gifted with two Thompson seedless grape vines. They grow beautifully each year and put on a few grapes, but not as many as I'd like. I suspect that I'm not trimming them properly, but I'm unsure of the correct way and time of year. I'm also unsure of how much water they need. I would appreciate any advice you could give me concerning their care.

A. When we buy fruit crops for our home gardens, we often look at varieties that we are familiar with from the grocery store. Thus we see a lot of Thompson seedless grapes, Bartlett pears and red delicious apples in home gardens. These aren't always the best varieties for our climate. However, you have them now, so let's try to make the most of your planting. Table grapes need to be pruned hard every year in February. We normally count buds on the vines, leaving a minimum of 10 buds for young vines and a maximum of 60 buds for older more vigorous vines. Each bud can produce at least a cluster of grapes. If you don't prune enough, table grapes tend to ripen one grape at a time in the cluster, instead of the whole cluster ripening. Water when dry throughout the growing season and monitor for insects and diseases and spray accordingly. If you want to replant with an easier care grape, consider one of the varieties developed by the UA System Division of Agriculture such as Reliance, Mars or Venus.

Q. I live in Pendleton (10 miles from Dumas). I was wondering if we can raise cherry trees here.

A. Cherry trees do grow in Arkansas, but they are a bit difficult to grow in our climate, and often birds get more of the fruit than the grower. Tart cherries are a bit easier to grow in Arkansas (especially south Arkansas) than sweet cherries. The sweet cherries are more prone to diseases and cracking, plus are less tolerant of heat and humidity. The new cultivars of tart cherries are all self-fruitful, so you only need one tree to have a crop. Choose a variety that is small enough to allow for protective bird netting to keep birds at bay.

Q. Our four rows of blackberries are about 6 years old, and we mulch them with composted wood chips the tree trimmers dump on our property. Many of them have large nodular growths at the soil line on their stems, which eventually will kill the plant. I haven't found anything similar in the extension's online disease library. We are going to pull them out and start all over. What is the disease, does it remain in the soil (we are moving to a different planting location) and what treatment might prevent it? Also, I've been hearing about new blackberry varieties out of the U of A, do you have any suggestions as to which ones are best for home production?

A. Two possibilities come to my mind, based on the description: crown gall, which is a bacterial disease or crown borer, which is an insect. For an accurate diagnosis, submit a section of the lower stem with roots and soil attached to your local extension office so they can send it to the disease diagnostic lab. As for varieties of blackberries, see this chart of the Arkansas recommended varieties: www.uaex.edu/yard-garden/fruits-nuts/berries.aspx. I personally love the thornless ones; Apache is my favorite.

AUGUST

Banana peppers

Tomato hornworm

IF YOU HAVE ALREADY HARVESTED and some of your vegetables have played out, this is the time to replant for a fall harvest. Water and mulch will make your job easier, but monitor for insects and diseases. Mulch is a vital part of any garden right now. Mulch not only keeps the weeds down, it also helps moderate soil temperature and moisture, all of which are needed throughout an Arkansas summer. There are numerous materials available: organic leaves, straw, bark, newspapers and plastic. If using a black plastic in your vegetable garden (and that is the only place it should be used) cover the black plastic with mulch during these hot days. Black plastic can help warm up the soil early in the season, but can make it almost too hot when temperatures are at their highest. Shredded leaves or newspaper placed over the plastic can cool it down some.

Now is the time to clean up spent vegetable gardens and consider solarization, or at least planting a cover crop. Good sanitation can do wonders for a garden spot. Every year, more and more gardeners mention problems with their tomatoes. If planted in the same spot year after year, diseases build up and hit the plants earlier and earlier. Solarization is a process that is best done in August, but September can still be a hot month, so it is worth the effort. Till the garden spot as thoroughly as possible, wet it heavily and then cover with clear plastic, making sure there is firm contact between soil and plastic. Leave the treated area covered for at least 6 weeks. If you are done for the year, leave it covered all winter and then plant next spring. If the season hasn't gotten the best of you, there is still time to plant some fall crops. August is an excellent month to plant your fall garden, but do remember that fall gardens require diligence in keeping diseases and insects away. Water will be a huge factor as well. Mulching the garden can keep down weeds and help to conserve moisture. You can plant broccoli, cabbage, greens, carrots and kale for cool-season plants, and if you can find a few more tomatoes and pepper plants, they can bear until a frost. Lettuce, spinach, Swiss chard and radishes can also be planted. Water these plants well and mulch to get them established.

HARVEST

HEAT AND HUMIDITY are not great gardening companions, but those are the conditions Arkansas has to offer. Try to get your gardening chores done early in the day. The peak summer vegetable gardening season is near its end, and none too soon for many gardeners. For gardens that are still producing, try to harvest vegetables early in the day before the heat takes its toll. Most fruits and vegetables taste better if harvested before the heat of the day has set in. Herbs are best harvested in the morning after any dew has dried but before the heat of the day sets in. Many vegetable gardens slow down production in the heat. Okra, sweet potatoes and southern peas are in their element and thriving, but often tomatoes take a breather and stop setting fruit when temperatures exceed 90 to 95 degrees during the day, or stay above 75 degrees at night. Keep your plants alive and they will rebound as things cool off.

Knowing what to look for can ensure that you get the most from your garden. Sweet corn is ripe when the silks begin to turn brown and dry. Take a peek at one or two of the ears by pulling back the shuck and pressing into a kernel or two. If the corn gives off a milky liquid and the ear is fully formed, harvest them. The quicker you can go from garden to table, the sweeter the corn will be. Cantaloupes and watermelons tend to be at their sweetest if it is a bit on the dry side during harvest. Too much rainfall dilutes the sugars. When cantaloupes are ripe, the stems should easily separate from the vine, the fruits should develop a light tan webbing pattern and the blossom end should be slightly soft and smell like cantaloupe. Ripe watermelons will have a dry curly brown tendril at stem end, a dullish sheen on the fruit and a white to yellow underbelly. Keep picking your cucumbers as they mature, as letting old fruit stay on the vines will slow down future production. Fresh okra is best picked when small, no larger than 2 to 3 inches. The bigger they get, the tougher the pods are.

Many of you may feel permanently attached to a garden hose, but plants in containers must be watered daily. The main goal for gardening in the peak of summer is to keep plants healthy and alive, and water is the key to success. Whether plants are in the ground or in containers, ample water is the key to their livelihood.

There is no easy formula that works for every yard. Some gardens have deep, rich soil while others have shallow, rocky sites, so water retention varies. Amount of sun, type of plants growing, soil and slope are all variables that alter water needs. Learn what works in your yard. Find a day when it is a bit cooler and give your container plants some water-soluble fertilizer. Frequent watering leaches nutrition and many plants can use a shot in the arm. However, fertilizer is a salt and can burn plants that are already dry and heat-stressed. Use the fertilizer after you have watered and do so early in the day to avoid damage. Also, go lightly–light, frequent applications would be better than a heavy dose. Be careful when using pesticides, and use caution even when applying fertilizers. Heat and drought-stressed plants are more susceptible to damage, even with products that are labeled for use now. When temperatures get extremely high, coupled with dry conditions, plants often look for moisture in any available form. If a pesticide is needed, try to do so early or late in the day–avoid mid-day applications when temperatures are at their highest. Make sure plants have ample moisture before any such applications. Work smart for your plants, but it is also easier on you to avoid the peak, mid-day sun.

Plant of the Month

Eggplant

Solanum Melongena

EGGPLANTS WERE NOT common in gardens or kitchens until the past decade or so. Now, for many of us, they are a staple. Eggplants belong to the nightshade family, which includes tomatoes, peppers and potatoes. Unlike tomatoes, eggplants thrive in the hottest parts of summer, continuing to set fruit even on hot, humid days. They grow on a short, stalky bush similar to peppers and rarely need staking, although if your plants get taller and are loaded with fruit, added support would be welcome.

Most people are familiar with the larger fruited varieties such as Black Beauty, but the Oriental varieties–Ichiban, with the long, tapered fruits–are gaining ground. In addition, there are small egg-shaped varieties in mature shades of white, yellow and orange, along with striped and spotted varieties.

All eggplants need warm conditions to grow, so don't plant too early in the spring, allowing the soil temperatures to warm up. Eggplants will continue to grow, bloom and set fruit until the really cool days of fall. The main pest problem is the flea beetle, which can cause small holes in the leaves and a stippling effect on the fruit.

While eggplants can be harvested from small-sized fruits up to larger ones, under-ripe or over-ripe fruits can be a bit bitter. For the larger-fruited forms, the outer rind will be deep, dark purple and have shiny skin. If the skin begins to turn dull or the color begins to fade, they are getting too ripe. The smaller-fruited forms will usually stop growing larger and the outer skin will get glossy. Although we have all done it, try not to pull the mature fruits off by hand, since they are firmly attached and you can damage the plant. Use pruning shears to harvest and leave a short stem attached. Eggplants will last for about a week in the refrigerator and can be grilled, fried, sautéed or roasted. If you start having too many to eat at once, roast them along with peppers, garlic and tomatoes in the oven, then puree in the blender for an outstanding dip.

Q & A

Q. We have approximately 30 blueberry bushes we planted about 8 years ago and they are producing beautifully. We have just gotten them well established and now we are moving. The new owners are planning to build in the spot they are planted. Is it possible to move blueberry bushes to our new location?

A. Almost any plant can be moved with a little bit of time and care. If at all possible, wait until the plants go dormant, so you can prune and move at the same time. If there is any distance involved in the move, make sure the root system is protected from temperature extremes and drying wind and sun. Have the new site prepared well in advance. Make sure it is well drained and acidic–have the soil tested and correct as needed prior to planting. Build up your beds and have ample mulch and moisture ready. Try to get the plants back in the ground as soon as possible. I would not try to move them when it is this hot and dry, but if fall is not possible, move as late as you can and pot them up for the transport.

Q. I planted a winter squash this year, butternut squash, for the first time. Some of the squash are getting fairly large now but are still green. How do you know when the squash are ready for harvest?

A. Butternut squash will typically turn a light tan or buff color when mature. As with all winter squashes, they will have a hard outer rind when mature. They are a long-season crop, usually taking about 90 days to mature. When they are fully mature, they store quite well, or can be eaten when harvested.

Q. We have a 15 foot by 18 foot fig tree. It's produced a marvelous amount of figs this year, but needs to be trimmed back. It's still producing a few small figs. Any suggestions about how much to cut them back and when? We, the birds and raccoons love it.

A. Figs bear their fruit on the current season growth. The best time to prune them is right before they start growing in the spring. Figs can suffer winter damage, and many years were frozen back by one half or more. That hasn't been the case in the past 10 years or so, and now the figs are becoming trees, instead of bushes, but we still want them to get through the winter before pruning. Pruning can be done if they are intruding into other areas, but if there is room for the large size I recommend leaving them tall. Let the top figs go for the birds and you can harvest the lower section.

Q. I have a question concerning Indian peach trees. I purchased some from a man in Clinton. How do you take care of them? Are they self-pollinating or do you have to have two? I was going to give one to my son and my sister, but I might need to give them two.

A. Peaches in general are self-fruitful, so one tree should be enough for production. The Indian peach is an old-fashioned variety, with many fans. It can have the same insect and disease problems as other peaches, so a thorough spray schedule is advised. You can get a copy of the spray guide for home orchards from your local county extension office. Make sure you plant the peaches in full sun and well-drained soil. Prune them every year in late February.

Q. I am planning on planting some peach trees. I would like to know the best time of year to set them out. I want a variety starting with early peaches and ending with the latest harvest period. I have been told that Haven varieties would be good to consider. I live in western Little Rock on a hillside and I think the hill would be a good place to grow fruit.

A. The absolute best time in my opinion to plant trees of any sort–be they fruiting or ornamental–is fall, from late October through early December. As they are going into dormancy, they have all winter and early spring to get their root system established and are stronger for their first growing season in the ground. The only limitation with fall planting is that sometimes variety selection is down, since most nurseries get their shipment of fruit trees in Februrary. If you can't find what you are looking for, then early spring is your next best bet. While many gardeners want peaches, peach trees are the hardest fruit for home gardeners to grow, since they are prone to many insect and disease issues.

Q. What causes eggplant fruit to become misshapen and oddly colored?

A. Poor-quality eggplant fruit is generally associated with low moisture and high temperature conditions. Over-mature eggplant fruit will become dull-colored and will often develop a bronze appearance. For maximum production, remove the eggplant fruit before it is fully mature to allow additional fruit to develop.

Q. This spring I put out some 3-year roots of asparagus. I went by the book and they have done well. Now I have nice big ferns (the cat likes to sit under there and look the world over), but come fall, I do not know what I am supposed to do with the ferns. Do I cut them down before I bed the ground for their winter nap?

A. There are two schools of thought for the ferny growth. Most people cut off the dead fronds as soon as we've had a killing frost, while others leave them for the bulk of the winter to keep weeds at bay, cleaning up the bed in late January in preparation for the growing season. The ferns are what manufacture the food during the growing season for good asparagus spear production in the spring. You should be able to harvest next spring, since your plants will actually be 4 years old.

Q & A

Q. I need to know when to plant my turnip and collard greens for fall.

A. You can begin planting greens in August and plant new rows weekly through September. Unless we have an extremely brutal winter, they should overwinter nicely and you can harvest greens all winter and spring.

Q. I planted a red delicious apple tree in my yard several years ago. It grows well, and I prune it in the spring as needed. I have even begun a spray program for insects and diseases, but I have gotten no apples. How long does it take to produce apples, and is there anything I can do to insure a good crop?

A. Apple trees need another variety of apple tree planted nearby to cross pollinate with. That may be one of your problems. If it is a standard variety versus a dwarf tree, it can take up to eight to 10 years to produce apples, while a dwarf tree can begin producing in three to five years.

Q. I have two problems with my tomatoes. First, around the first of June, the plants began to turn brown at the bottom and worked up to the top. Second, for the last two weeks as the tomatoes ripened, they split open and are not edible. They were heavily fertilized during their first month of planting and get plenty of water. The plants are 7 feet tall and about 5 feet across and have been and still are loaded with tomatoes. We have had an excellent crop but they are the largest plants that I have ever seen. I might add that they are in a rose bed and are exposed to rose fungicide spray. Any idea as to why they are splitting and why they turned brown?

Split tomato

A. Your tomatoes have two physiological problems, not diseases. The first one is blossom end rot. It is a calcium deficiency, caused by fluctuation of moisture levels. We often see a huge amount of blossom end rot when we have a heavy rain following a dry period. The best you can do for this problem is to add a little lime to the planting soil and mulch the plants to help keep the soil as uniformly moist as possible. Don't overdo it with fertilizer.

The problem you are now having with cracking is also a moisture problem. When tomatoes reach a mature fruit size, the outer skin begins to thicken. If they get a lot of water after this stage, they try to grow some more, and the outer skin cracks. Try to keep moisture levels as constant as possible, avoiding huge swings from dry to wet. It doesn't hurt the fruit to eat it after cracking, but it can cause the fruits to decay more quickly. Some varieties are more susceptible to cracking than others, especially the larger fruited varieties. I am concerned with their exposure to rose fungicides because unless you have a product that specifically lists edibles, many ornamental fungicides are only labeled for ornamentals. You should not be spraying anything edible unless the pesticide is labeled for their use. Remember, the label is the law. Try to separate edibles from ornamentals that need spraying.

Q. Can pomegranate plants be grown in Arkansas? My grandmother had one with bright orange blooms but it never produced anything edible. I would love to grow my own pomegranates but I was wondering if I would ever get any fruit?

A. Pomegranates (*Punica granatum*) have seen a huge surge in popularity as one of the super fruits. Pomegranates are native to the Middle East and were brought to the U.S. by early Spanish settlers. Pomegranates have been grown as an ornamental plant for years in Arkansas with very showy orange blooms. Many set small fruit, but with our humid summers, rarely do we see great fruit production. Today, a new series of Russian pomegranates have shown good results with fruiting and winter hardiness. They need full sun and a well-drained soil. Pomegranates flower on new growth, much like a fig, so if any pruning is needed, it should be done before new growth begins in late February to early March. The fruit is produced on short spurs found on 2- to 3-year-old stems. Light annual pruning will encourage new fruiting spurs to develop, but avoid heavy pruning which can reduce fruiting.

Q. Can I use store-bought new potatoes to use as seed potatoes to plant in my vegetable garden?

A. While it isn't recommended, if you plan to have a late crop of potatoes, seed potatoes are usually not available when it is time to plant. It is too late to plant potatoes, or too early. They are best planted in late February through early April and then again in mid-July through August for a fall harvest. Keep in mind that potatoes bought at the grocery store are typically treated to prevent sprouting. I have had some gardeners who planted some potatoes that had begun to sprout in their kitchen, and they had decent results, but they usually struggled with disease issues. You can save some spring garden potatoes to use in a fall planting. Newly harvested potatoes have a natural dormancy, that prevents them from sprouting quickly, so you may want to make sure they are stored in a cool, dry place for a month or two before planting.

SEPTEMBER

Lettuce seedlings

WE OFTEN HAVE A SUMMER of extremes–wet and dry, cool and hot, and all parts in between. We are in the home stretch for hot weather gardening, but don't throw in the towel just yet. September is notorious for teasing us with a day or two of mild weather and then bouncing back with extreme heat. Continue to pay attention to water needs and continue to plant for late-season color and harvest.

September usually gives us a break in the heat and dry conditions, with much needed rain almost statewide. Rainfall can be spotty, but it helps green things up and gets our gardens ready for winter. It is important to monitor the rainfall (or lack thereof) in your yard and water as needed.

Vegetable gardening continues to gain in popularity and how we garden has changed. We can now grow edible plants year-round with just a little extra protection in the winter months. Cool season gardening has great advantages since there are much fewer insects and diseases, and weeds are not as challenging–especially if you mulch. So if you thought it was time to harvest and put the garden to bed, think again. Continue to harvest summer crops, but plan for a fall and winter garden.

Start planting lettuce, broccoli, cabbage, spinach and greens. Many garden centers are now selling a good selection of vegetable plants and seeds for fall and winter gardening. Establishing fall vegetable gardens can be a bit challenging due to the large numbers of insects that are around and the hot, humid weather of early fall. With a little diligence, plenty of water and mulch, you can have a great fall garden. Monitor for pests early and control them as needed. Once the weather cools off, problems taper off,

Parsley

as well. If you don't have a stand-alone garden, consider planting edible kale and cabbage with pansies instead of the ornamental varieties. Parsley and cilantro are a great addition to the fall garden, as well as Swiss chard, bull's blood beets and purple mustard. All of these are as showy as they are good to eat! If some instant color in the landscape is needed, pumpkins and gourds are popping up at garden centers statewide.

In addition to vegetables in the garden, herbs are a great addition. Whether you grow them in containers, intersperse them with your ornamentals, plant them in the vegetable garden or plant a stand-alone herb garden, they are easy to grow and use in cooking. Know if they are annuals or perennials. Annual herbs, such as basil, need to be used frequently to keep them bushy and bloom-free. The end of their growing season is near, so keep using them. If you harvest more than you can use at one sitting, dry them and use later or mix some with water and freeze in ice cube trays. Dried herbs can be added to soups and stews all winter. In the case of basil, make some pesto for use this winter. If you are growing perennials, including rosemary, sage, thyme and oregano, don't overharvest when the weather is hot and dry. Also, don't over-prune them late in the season. We don't want to encourage a lot of new tender growth too late in the year, nor head into cold weather too exposed. Now is a good time to start planting cilantro and parsley for cool weather. Both of these plants thrive in the cooler days of fall and winter. Hard freezes may burn cilantro more than parsley, but with minimum protection they can grow all winter long.

Gourd

HARVEST

IF THE IDEA OF PLANTING more is too much for you, harvest what is left and consider planting a cover crop or green manure crop. Planting now will give a good cover all winter, prevent weeds from establishing themselves and add great nitrogen-rich organic matter in the spring. Rye, crimson clover, vetch, oats and buckwheat can all be planted in September. Till them into the soil about a month before you plan to plant your garden the following spring.

The end of the gardening season also offers plenty of material for composting. Avoid using plant debris that was diseased. While a good compost pile should get hot enough to kill the diseased organisms, a home pile often fails to distribute the heat uniformly throughout the pile and may not kill all the organisms.

Plant of the Month

Luffa Gourd

Cucurbitoideae Luffinae

LUFFA GOURDS ARE ALSO REFERRED to as the dishcloth or sponge gourd, since they are typically grown to produce your own "sponges." Much like most other gourds, the luffa variety are quite vigorous and the vines can spread 20 feet or more. While they can be grown on the ground, it is best to grow them on a sturdy trellis or fence to conserve space and to get straight fruits.

Most gardeners grow luffa gourds to use the fibrous insides as a sponge. However, the young fruits that are 6 inches or less in size can be cooked and eaten as squash or substituted for cucumber in salads, and are sometimes sold as Chinese okra in their edible form.

Luffa gourds are a member of the *cucurbita* family, along with cucumbers, squash, watermelons and cantaloupes. Like all members of that family, they have separate male and separate female flowers on the same plant. Pollinators are needed to transfer pollen from the male bloom to the female bloom. The plants like warm soils, so don't plant gourds before May. These gourds establish rather quickly when the temperatures are warm. The luffa gourd can be used as an annual screen, with large leaves and showy yellow blooms. The developing fruits look a bit like a large zucchini or

cucumbers, eventually reaching a length of 2 feet. They remain green until they're thoroughly ripe. When the gourds are ripe, their skins will dry and the stems will turn yellow. Allow luffas to mature on the vines if you can. Full-size fruits that are still green produce soft, fine-textured sponges that don't last as long as the dried ones. Prior to a killing frost, harvest all sizes and see what you can get.

Once you harvest the ripe gourds, dry them before peeling off the outer skin to get to the sponge. Once dry, cut open the larger end of the gourd and shake out the seeds. Seeds can be saved to replant the following summer, but let them dry for a few days before storing. Mature, dry fruit will peel somewhat easily, while green fruit can be a bit more of a challenge. Some gardeners peel the skin off while they are dry, while others soak the gourds in warm water for a few hours or overnight and then peel. Once sponges are loose, let them air dry in the sun to help them turn white. They can then be used as a sponge in your bath or kitchen. They can also make great gifts, along with a few seeds folks could use to plant their own next year!

Q & A

Q. This is the first year I grew asparagus with 2-year-old crowns. I did not harvest any this year as directed. What or how do I take care of them this winter? When I harvest next year how much and how often? How do I take care of my garden spot for the winter as I have never had a designated garden spot before?

A. Asparagus is a great perennial vegetable. You can begin a small harvest next spring, but don't overdo it. Harvest until the size of the spears is smaller than a pencil in diameter. If you continue to harvest really small spears, you can wear the plant out, which will impact your harvest for years to come. By the following year, you should be in full production. As for winter care, simply let the ferny fronds grow until a killing frost and then cut them back. Some folks leave the fronds out for the bulk of the winter to cut down on weed issues, but you should remove the spent tops by mid-January at the latest to get the spot ready for spring harvest. For the general garden, fall sanitation–removing spent debris and either mulching or planting a fall cover crop–can help keep weeds at bay and start your season cleaner. Some choices for fall cover crops include clovers, vetches, rye and field peas.

Q. I did not know you could plant vegetables this late in the year, but my neighbor just planted some. I love turnips and the greens. Can I still plant them now?

A. Now is a great time to plant fall vegetables. The weather usually begins to show some signs of fall with cooler temperatures and some rain, so the seeds should take off and give us a wonderful fall and winter harvest. While we grow turnips and collards by seed, vegetable transplants for broccoli, cabbage and other cool-season vegetables have arrived at garden centers.

Q. We are a bit stumped at a plant that came up in our garden. For a long time, we thought it was a honeydew melon, but I cut one, and it had the flavor of a cucumber. Is it a squash that has grown larger than it should have? There were only two of these on the entire plant, and both fruits grew very large.

A. The leaves look more like a watermelon. Did the plant grow from a seed left over from last year? If so, it could be a cross between a cucumber, squash, watermelon, etc., members of the cucurbit family will cross pollinate and the resulting seeds can give you some pretty interesting fruits. It should be safe to eat, and you may like the flavor, or not. If you home compost, often the seeds that are in the remains begin to sprout in the garden or compost pile.

Q. We moved to a new home about a year ago and it had an apple tree in the yard. This spring it bloomed and small apples began to grow. After the apples were about walnut size, I noticed a few

brown spots on some of them. After about a week, half the apples appeared rotten. Eventually all the apples did the same. I don't know what kind of apple tree this is, or how old it is. It's around 20 feet high. Do you know why this happened? Should I have sprayed it with something?

A. Apples and pears tend to be more forgiving than peaches and plums when it comes to insect and disease issues, but if you want blemish free large fruits, you need to follow a spray schedule. There are numerous diseases and insects which can attack. You can find the extention's home fruit spray schedule here: www.uaex.edu/publications/pdf/FSA-7503.pdf. They also need to be pruned annually as well.

Q. We have 3 apple trees planted very closely to each other. The apples on one of the trees (the only Winesap) have begun to split open. The apples on all of the trees are healthy, except for the splitting. This has occurred for several years. What could be the cause and what is the remedy?

A. Apples splitting is similar to tomatoes splitting–it is a problem with water. When it is really dry and we get a downpour, the water pressure changes inside the fruit and some fruits split. Thinner-skinned apples are more susceptible than thicker-skinned fruits. The only recourse you have is to keep the trees mulched and to try to moderate the moisture levels. If the fruits are ripe, you can eat them, but do so quickly as they deteriorate fast once they split.

Q. I would appreciate any advice in regards to insects, fertilizing and watering of my outdoor plants. I live in the country and have 8 acres. I have apple, pear and plum trees. Each plant seems to have different requirements. I find myself watering all the above every other day. I fertilize at the appropriate times and spray for insects (preventive, systemic) and diseases. My apple tree didn't flower this year. Instead, it developed rust spots. My plum tree had one flower on it and the pear tree had about 10 fruits. These three trees are about 2 to 3 years old. My soil is a mixture of dirt, sand and clay. I amend the soil each time I plant something new. I guess what I'm asking is: Once a plant is established, is it necessary to water like I'm watering? If I don't, the plants appear to stress. Also, how do I control my insect problem? I fear that this year I may have over-used some products and killed the good insects and left the plants prey to opportunistic insects and diseases. Help, please.

A. One thing to be aware of is that frequent watering makes plants demand more, because it encourages shallow roots. Infrequent, deep watering encourages a deeper root zone. However, every yard is different. Yards with rocky soil, steep slopes and full sun require more water than level yards with great soil.

You have also picked some pretty needy plants. Fruit trees require quite a bit of maintenance, including spray schedules and watering. They also often don't begin to bear fruit well until they are 5 to 8 years old. Mulching is

Q & A

also something that I would strongly encourage. It helps to retain moisture and moderates the soil temperature. Gradually wean them from their daily water needs by applying more water when you do water, and applying it less often. It isn't something you can reverse overnight. Many people with automatic sprinkler systems make this mistake. Monitor for insects and diseases and spray as needed. For the fruit trees, preventative sprays are often best.

Q. I have what I believe to be some kind of pear. The fruit is small, about the size of a ping pong ball, but the texture and flesh very much resemble a pear, as do the leaf and limbs. What do you think it is? The reason for the inquiry is that there are three of these trees along the Arkansas River and the deer like to camp out around them endlessly searching for dropping fruit. If you know what this tree is, could you possibly tell me where I could purchase some of them or if the seed might be viable?

A. You will find many seedling ornamental pears around the state. The Bradford pear and other ornamental pears are all selections of the Callery pear (*Pyrus calleryana*). Fruit size can vary from the size of a BB to a large crabapple. When the birds drop the seeds, there is a great deal of variability in the resulting seedling pear. While deer may flock to them, and probably birds and squirrels, these seedling pears are becoming a nuisance plant–quite invasive. You will also find that many of these seedlings and larger trees have thorns on them, too. I would not recommend planting any more ornamental pear trees in Arkansas.

Q. I need information on when and how to prune apple trees. I have some in my backyard and have never attempted this. These varieties are approximately 5 years old.

A. Apple trees should be pruned every year, from the first year they are in the ground to every year thereafter. Since your trees have not been pruned in 5 years, chances are very good that they need some major pruning. You probably have numerous branches that are crossing over and through the tree, as well as those that are drooping downward. You need to do general shaping to keep the tree at a manageable height for picking. Most apple trees are pruned with a central leader system–sort of like a Christmas tree, with the center branch the tallest, and subsequent branches lower than that. Pruning of fruit trees should be done while they are dormant. Most home gardeners wait until late February to do the pruning. Your local county extension office has a good fact sheet on how to prune.

Q. I live in Scott and have a nests of worms in my pecan tree. Is there something that we can spray on the trees? When should we spray? How often? Is it safe on pecan trees?

A. You have a nice case of fall webworms. In the spring, we get tent caterpillars for a few weeks, but in mid- to late summer we start with fall webworms, and we can have several generations per season. The webs are a tad

unsightly, but there is very little damage that occurs to the trees. With webworms, they feed inside the web, making the web larger over time. They primarily eat the leaves, and this late in the year, that doesn't hurt the trees–look at how many leaves are already falling. If you really dislike them, you can try to use a high-powered spray at the end of your hose and spray with BT (*Bacillus thuringiensis*), an organic spray. The key is to spray around the web and into it, getting the spray on the leaves. The caterpillars have to eat the foliage to ingest the BT for it to work. If you have small trees with webs close to the ground, you can use a rake and pull the webs out of the tree and dispose of them, but don't hurt yourself trying to climb up into the tree to remove them, and don't use the old-fashioned method of burning them out of the trees, or you can damage your trees, not to mention hurt yourself. The insects (or the BT) will not affect the safety of the pecans themselves. While webworms can attack a wide range of tree species, pecans are one of their favorites. But look on the bright side, Halloween is just around the corner, and you could pretend they are Halloween decorations–they look a bit spooky!

Q. I brought a young lemon tree back from Florida and over-wintered it. After I put it outside in a large pot, full sun, it produced about a dozen lemons. So far, these lemons are still very green, and have not grown much bigger than their initial growth. When should they start to ripen, and should they have increased in size by now? The plant is watered regularly and has good drainage. I would appreciate some information so that we can eventually taste our lemons!

A. Lemons can bear fruit and ripen in Arkansas, but they are normally not winter hardy. If they have not started changing color by early to mid-October, move the plants indoors to a bright, sunny area. The fruit should eventually ripen. The most common variety of lemon sold for container gardening is the Meyer lemon and it will produce good quality fruits, they just can't take our winters.

OCTOBER

HOPEFULLY THE LAST of the hot, dry weather is now behind us and we can move into fall. Leaves are falling in earnest and trees are beginning to put on their fall show. We get the best array of fall colors when we have warm days and cool nights coupled with ample moisture. Some trees have shed their leaves early without turning color, but we are seeing a good display on others, and there is still time to have more. As leaves fall, rake them up and, if you can, shred them for use in a compost pile or mulch. Shredded leaves will break down much more easily than if you leave them whole.

Garden clean-up is important. Our poor plants need as much tender loving care as they can get after making it through hot months outside. Remove dying plants and rake up spent debris. Add a fresh layer of mulch in the garden. Take inventory of what worked and what didn't. Continue to fertilize winter vegetable gardens. Check for insects.

Vegetable gardening doesn't need end with the coming of cooler weather. Many gardeners are using row covers or hoop houses to continue to grow year-round. In a milder season, greens, cabbage, broccoli and chard overwinter without additional covering. The type of winter we have will determine how much protection is needed. If you haven't planted yet, consider planting edible cabbage and kale instead of the ornamental cabbage and kale in your flower beds. You can also find bulls blood beets, giant mustard and Swiss chard that can give you beautiful winter color, and is edible to boot. If you do not plan on a fall vegetable garden, don't leave the spot bare all winter or you will end up with a great crop of weeds. There is still time to plant cool-season vegetable transplants like cabbage, broccoli. Turnip, mustard greens and kale can take fairly cold temperatures and can serve as a cover crop or an edible. Plant them as soon as possible or seeds may not have enough time to get established before the weather turns cold. If you are done with edibles for the year, cover the garden with either a green manure crop, cover crop or put down a thick layer of mulch–shredded leaves, compost, etc. This can keep the weeds at bay and you can work this organic matter in when you till the garden next spring.

HARVEST

COMPOST SEASON IS IN FULL SWING with all the raw materials available, from leaves to grass clippings and spent vegetable plants. With so many raw materials to work with, this is a composter's nirvana now. Remember, you need a combination of green and brown matter to make it work. Vegetable scraps, coffee grounds and fruit peelings work well, but avoid adding any meat or dairy products to the compost pile. If you can shred the materials before you add them, it will speed up the composting process. If plants died because of drought or have simply finished producing, add those to the pile. If plants were heavily diseased or loaded with insects, don't put them in the compost. Although a compost pile does heat up and can kill many disease organisms, insects and weed seeds, a home compost pile doesn't have great uniform heat throughout the pile and won't kill all the bad stuff. How many of you have used compost and had tomatoes and unusual gourds or squash emerging? This is from seeds that made it through, and while they aren't bad seeds, the pigweeds and nutsedge are.

Practice good sanitation in the garden. As plants begin to play out, pull them up and get them out of the garden. Weeds are continuing to grow and if you allow them to bloom and set seeds, you will have more next season. Summer weeds are nearing the end of their season while winter weeds are beginning to grow. That is one thing we are almost never without in a garden: weeds! Use a good hoe, or hand pull, mow and mulch.

Plant of the Month

Pumpkins

Cucurbita pepo

OCTOBER AND PUMPKINS are almost synonymous. From the tiny Jack-be-little to the competition-sized giants of county fairs, a wide variety of pumpkins are readily available at local markets. Groupings of pumpkins, gourds and Indian corn can add interest and color to the fall garden. When choosing your fall art, make sure the pumpkins still have a small stem. If they don't have a stem or if they have any soft spots, they can rot fairly easily. The same goes for gourds with any soft spots or blemishes. If you choose wisely, these fall vegetables can grace your garden through the winter holidays. If you do plan to carve your

pumpkin for Halloween, do so no sooner than the day before as they break down quickly once cut. Many people have asked me if they can save the seeds to plant next season. The answer is yes, but probably not a wise move. Pumpkin seeds will not breed true, so what you get next season may be quite different. Experiment if you want to take a chance, but if you want something identical, plant new seeds and roast this year's to eat!

In years past most families bought one pumpkin to carve for Halloween, but today they are used as an ornamental staple in the fall garden with clusters of pumpkins, gourds, hay bales and corn stalks serving as the focal element. Pumpkins in all sizes and shapes, from the traditional orange to white, red, green and striped; smooth rinds to warty. While pumpkins aren't difficult to grow, they do require a long time to mature, so many people choose to simply let someone else grow them and buy them each fall.

Pumpkins are members of the cucurbit family, which means they are kissing cousins of cucumbers, squash, watermelons and gourds. They are normally planted in the garden once the soil warms up in June or early July, which which means they will be ready for a fall harvest. Pumpkins are vining plants and require quite a bit of space to produce. Sizes range from the tiny Jack-b-little which produce a softball size fruit up, to the giant, award-winners like Big Max and Prize Winner, which can produce fruits weighing more than

100 pounds. Supposedly, the world record is over 1800 pounds for a pumpkin. These giant fruits aren't that attractive, but they do break records.

Pumpkins have been found in records dating all the way back to Peru in 2000 B.C. and were definitely a staple in the diet of Native Americans. The tradition of carving a pumpkin and lighting it with a candle dates back to the Celtic people. In those days, a common tradition each fall was a harvest bonfire, symbolizing the end of summer. Families would carry an ember from this fire to light their own fire at home. The traditional mode of transportation for the ember was a hollowed-out turnip. They began to carve faces into their turnips to ward off evil spirits. After the potato famine and the migration to the new world, turnips were not as readily available, so pumpkins became the fruit of choice. In recent years, what most of us remember from our childhood as simple faces carved into the pumpkin have been transformed into works of art. While pumpkin carving is still a family tradition, simply stacking pumpkins in the landscape, bordering beds or clustering them with mums and pansies, makes them an ornamental plant as well as a utilitarian one.

Pumpkins as a food source are more commonly known in can-form for pumpkin pies during the holiday, but pumpkins can be roasted and served as a vegetable. You can even cook the whole pumpkin and make your own pie filling. Pie pumpkins are traditionally smaller fruited forms, usually between three to six pounds. Pumpkins are low in calories, fat and sodium, and are also high in fiber. They are good sources of Vitamin A, Vitamin B, potassium, protein and iron. You can even cook a stew or soup inside a hollowed out pumpkin and then roast it in the oven. The flowers are also edible and roasted pumpkin seeds are a tasty snack.

If decoration is your main goal, choose a pumpkin with a stem attached. Look for one with a smooth rind free of soft spots or blemishes. If there is no stem, the fruit tends to deteriorate rather quickly. If you choose well, they can last for months, both inside and out. Some folks even paint them silver or gold to extend their usefulness. Another way to extend their life is to clean them and spray them with a clear paint.

You can use small pumpkins to border your flower beds or scatter them among your flowers. They can be hollowed out as serving bowls for a parties. Small ones can be strung together for garlands, wreaths or used as a candlestick holder. Keep in mind, the minute you cut a pumpkin, you shorten its shelf life.

A carved or cut pumpkin will only last a few days. Many choose to paint faces instead of carving one. But, why not do both? Get the whole family into the act.

Large or small, orange or white, decoration or food–or both!–tis the season for pumpkins!

Q&A

Q. I would like to plant a pecan tree. Can you give me any pointers?

A. Pecan trees are large trees at maturity and if you plan to harvest pecans, you need two different varieties for cross pollination. Nut trees typically take 7 to 10 years before they begin bearing nuts. Keep in mind that to produce quality pecans, you need to follow a regular spray schedule. Typically, mature pecan trees are so tall that it is hard for home gardeners to get thorough coverage. I tell home gardeners to consider pecan trees a shade tree and if they get quality nuts–and the squirrels don't beat you to them–that is a bonus.

Q. My pecan tree is very sick. It has knotty growths all over it. Please advise what is wrong with it and what can be done? This is the first year the tree has ever had blooms and it is 9 or 10 years old.

A. Your tree has a very common problem called phylloxera gall. Some years it is more prevalent than others. Three species of phylloxera are pecan pests, but only the Pecan Phylloxera causes economic damage in certain years. The pecan leaf phylloxera and the southern pecan leaf phylloxera feed primarily on the foliage, whereas the PP attacks the foliage, shoots and fruit and is therefore the most damaging. Phylloxera are small, aphid-like insect that are rarely seen, but the galls it produces are prominent and easily noticed. Severe infestations cause malformed, weakened shoots that finally die; such infestations can destroy entire limbs. The insect overwinters as eggs, which are in protected places on the branches of pecan trees. Soon after bud break, the eggs hatch and the young insects migrate to opening buds or leaf tissue to feed on the expanding new growth. Their feeding stimulates the development of galls or knotty growths. Eggs are then laid and hatched inside the galls, with the resulting nymphs remaining inside until they mature. In late June or early July, the galls split open and the mature nymphs emerge. Eggs are laid on protected parts of the trees and wait for next spring. Usually phylloxera galls are more a nuisance than a threat to the tree and timing is critical for control. The easiest method to reduce damage is to saturate as much of the trunk and lower limbs with a dormant or horticultural oil prior to bud break in the spring.

Q. We have some wild pecans growing in our yard and when we harvest the nuts they are bitter or have black rotten spots on the kernel. Is this an immune system problem of the trees that can be corrected with trace mineral supplements?

A. The problem is not nutritional, but an insect. Stink bugs attack the forming pecans and pierce the soft outer shell when it is forming. They leave behind small specks of saliva, which cause tiny, bitter black spots on the nuts. These can be cut out, the nuts are still edible. They can be controlled during the growing season with an insecticide spray schedule, but pecan trees produce such large trees that it is hard to get thorough spray coverage with home sprayers.

Q. I have "tame" blackberry bushes that are so happy that they are taking over the garden. I cut them back each fall to about 5 feet and try to remove all the old canes that I can. (Whew! What a job!) Could I cut them back more? This year they grew so tall that I fed most of the birds in the area because I couldn't reach the tops.

A. Blackberries can be kept pruned to a height of 4 to 5 feet to make them easier to pick next season. You may need to prune several times throughout the growing season to keep them in range. If you can remove the canes that bore the fruit as soon as you harvest, that could make your fall work a little less daunting. Blackberries bear fruit on 1-year-old wood. Once they bear, those canes die, but new canes grow amongst the old ones. Pruning them out before they totally die back allows the new canes room to grow. Keeping them pruned to a manageable height allows more branching and more fruit next year.

Q. I have a bed of asparagus that I would like to move. When is the proper time to move it and are there any precautions we need to take to insure its survival?

A. Move your asparagus this fall after the first killing frost, but begin preparing its new home now. Asparagus like a rich, humusy environment. Work manure, compost or similar organic matter into the soil and start killing grass and weeds. Then, when you are ready to move it, cut back the top fronds after frost kills them, dig the plants up and move them.

Blackberry

Q. I have a small backyard garden and plant broccoli and cabbage every spring and fall. I have done this for many years, but this past spring only a few plants headed. This fall, I have big and beautiful plants, but no heads. What am I doing wrong?

A. Do you have plenty of sunlight? At least 6 to 8 hours are needed to get them to head or set fruit. Cabbage takes longer to produce a large head than broccoli. Be patient and protect them if it gets well below 30 degrees, and they can continue to grow this winter. If you have deciduous trees, the leaves will soon fall completely and give your plants a bit more sunlight.

Q & A

Fig tree

Q. I have a fig tree that I transplanted several years ago to an area just under a large oak tree. It has put out leaves, but it hasn't produced any fruit or grown any at all. It was my mother's tree and I would like to keep it alive. What should I do?

A. Get out the shovel again and move the tree to a sunnier location. Figs must have at least 6 hours of sunlight per day to produce figs. Shade is keeping it from producing. Competition of the oak's root systems is probably keeping it from growing much. Move it to a protected spot on the east side of your house if possible. Fall is the ideal time to move it.

Q. We have recently moved to northeast Arkansas. We purchased topsoil this spring for our vegetable garden. We planted zucchini, as well as winter squash and pumpkins. We had big plants with big leaves and lots of flowers on long stems. There were many bees to pollinate. The vines, however, produced poorly. We had one pumpkin, a couple of winter squash and a few zucchini. Have you any idea why we didn't get more produce? Could you tell me where to go for garden information about this area?

A. It sounds like your plants were growing vegetatively instead of reproductively. This can be caused by several things. First, you must have a minimum of 6 to 8 hours of sunlight every day to produce these crops. If you have more shade, that could be the problem. The other cause could be that the soil is too rich or too high in nitrogen. This can cause plants to grow to the exclusion of fruiting. Cucurbits, which all of the plants you were growing are members of, produce both male and female flowers separately on the same plant. The male flowers are vegetative growth and will be produced even in the shade. They simply have a tall, straight stalk behind them. The female flowers have a small fruit behind them even before pollination. Once pollinated, this fruit continues to enlarge. It sounds like most of your blooms were male. Your local county extension service has a lot of great information on gardening for Arkansas. There is a whole series of vegetable fact sheets, including information on pumpkins and squash.

Q. Will trailing thyme grow around stepping stones? I need something that will stay alive all winter.

A. Creeping thyme is a wonderful ground cover around rocky sites. It doesn't like rich, wet areas, so it should do well around stepping stones and you get the added benefit of it being culinary as well as ornamental. There are actually several varieties of thyme with green, yellow or variegated foliage.

Q. For the past two years, I have planted squash in my garden, but all the plants do is bloom and I never get any squash. What is my problem and what can I do about it?

A. Does the area get enough sunlight? Keep in mind, that squash plants have separate male and female blooms. It can have male blooms even in partial shade. If you do have both blossoms and no fruit, it means you have no bees, or pollinators, which can transfer the pollen from the male blooms to the female blooms. You tell the difference in blooms by looking behind the flower. The females will have a tiny squash on them, while the males have a straight stem. Use care when applying insecticides so that you don't kill your bee population. If you can't get pollinators, you can play the part of the bee by manually transferring pollen using a paintbrush, but this can be tedious.

Q. My garden has been tilled, fertilized and weeded and now I want to cover it for winter. What kind of covering is best?

A. Solarizing soil with clear plastic to kill weeds, diseases and insects will only work during the months of July, August and September, or when it is hot outside. You can still use plastic to smother winter weeds and prevent them from growing this winter, but you would want to use black plastic to prevent light from getting through. Black plastic also warms up the soil earlier in the spring which can allow for earlier planting. Clear plastic used in the winter acts as a mini greenhouse and allows weeds to continue to grow.

Q. I would like to plant parsley this winter for extra color in my garden, but my seeds haven't come up. I figure we're getting too late now for the seedlings to even survive. What do you think?

A. Parsley is slow to germinate from seed. An old wives' tale claims the seeds go to the devil and back several times before they come up. Regardless of when they germinate, they wouldn't be able to be planted outside for at least 6 to 8 weeks. Then the winter temperatures would be too much for them. Why don't you continue to wait on your seedlings for a spring planting and buy some plants at a local nursery? That way you can get a full plant that can give you bright green color all winter long. Parsley looks great planted with pansies and other winter color.

Q. I still have lots of tomatoes this time of year and a lot of them split at the top. Got any idea why?

A. The splitting is caused by uneven moisture. When they get dry and then you water them–or we finally get a heavy rain–the fruits tend to split. Some varieties are more susceptible to this than others. For future reference, mulching does help.

NOVEMBER

Pine straw

DO A MAJOR FALL CLEANUP after a killing frost in both your flowerbeds and vegetable gardens. Cut back the fronds of asparagus as they die back and put down a light layer of mulch. If plants struggled with insects and diseases, rake up the spent debris and dispose of it. Don't add it to your compost pile or you may add more problems next season.

A light layer of leaves or pine needles on your lawn or garden is not an issue, but don't let them accumulate for too long. Heavy piles of leaves can cut down on air circulation, oxygen and sunlight. Consider using leaves for compost, as it is one of the best ways to enrich soil. Alternatively, use shredded leaves as mulch in the garden.

Mustard plant

Blueberries

If you haven't planted winter annuals, November is a good time to do so. Instead of planting pretty flowers alone, add edibles to your winter color mix and then you can have your plants and eat them, too! Pansies and violas are edible flowers, but consider planting edible kale and cabbage instead of flowering kale and cabbage. Swiss chard is showy all season and so are giant purple mustard, beets and bok choy. Parsley and cilantro can serve as a backdrop to flowering annuals, and all these plants can still be planted in cooler weather. The later you plant, the more important it is to buy blooming or larger plants. Small green plants typically won't flower much until spring if they are planted late, and we need to give them time to get a root system established before cold weather hits. If you planted winter annuals earlier in the season, continue to fertilize monthly to keep them growing and blooming.

November is the ideal month to plant blueberry bushes and fruit and nut trees, but sometimes the selection is not as good as it is in the spring. If you can find the plant varieties you like, start planting. Planting in cooler weather is easier on the plants. Since they are dormant (or will be soon), they can get busy establishing their root system without having to supply food and water to leaves and fruit.

HARVEST

How long your vegetable garden produces is dependent on when the first frost occurs and how cold it gets. Many of the cool-season vegetables can tolerate light frosts while warm-season vegetables die back quickly. If you kept your tomatoes and peppers alive during the dry months, they will still be producing. We are getting closer and closer to a killing frost. When you hear the prediction, harvest all tomatoes from the vines–both green and red. Put them in a single layer in a cardboard box or breathable container, and they will gradually ripen indoors. Or they can be individually wrapped in newspaper and stored in a cool, dry place. Take a few out each week and you can have fresh tomatoes for a month or longer.

Basil will not survive a frost either. If you have loads left, harvest it all. Don't be too severe in pruning perennial evergreen herbs this late in the season, but you can still use them.

Sweet potatoes must be harvested as soon after a frost as possible–if not before. They will rot quickly. Mulching carrots, turnips and beets can keep you in production for much of the winter season. The flavor of these vegetables is often much sweeter when harvested during cool weather, so continue to harvest your cool-season vegetables as needed.

If you want to harvest your edible ornamentals, be a bit judicious in how you cut them. You don't want to take off the whole plant or there will be nothing left to enjoy. Instead, prune foliage from around the base or lightly from around the plant. Clean up the garden as you harvest. Don't till plants back into the soil that have been infested with diseases or insects, or you may make your problems worse.

Sweet potatoes

With the use of season extenders, upended cardboard boxes, high tunnels or other devices, you can now continue to garden throughout the winter months. Pay attention to the weather and if temperatures are predicted to be well below freezing, cover cool-season vegetables. If you are using a plastic covering, pay attention to the forecast: sunny days can generate a lot of heat under plastic covering and your beds may need to be ventilated during the day and only covered at night.

Plant of the Month

Persimmon

Ebenaceae Diospyros

THE NATIVE PERSIMMON is a very adaptable tree, growing in most soil types in full sun to partial shade. Persimmon trees will withstand short periods of drought, but the fruit will be larger and of higher quality with regular watering. Extreme drought will cause the leaves and fruit to drop prematurely. At maturity, the tree can reach 40 feet. The persimmon is a cousin of the African ebony tree. It has hard, dark and beautifully grained wood. Many old trees were cut to make golf clubs during the early years of the 20th century and are still used in specialized furniture pieces.

Mature fruit may be yellow, orange, bright red or blue-black in color. When ripe, the fruit becomes soft and mushy. Unripe fruit, which is high in tannins, has a bitter, astringent flavor. The golden orange-to-red fruit are very sweet when fully ripened and astringency is reduced. When the fruit is ripe, it will pull away easily from the branch, turn a deep orange color and be soft to the touch.

Edible fruits often hang on the trees through fall and even into winter, unaffected by freezing temperatures. Songbirds, raccoons, squirrels and deer are some of the animals that enjoy the extra fruit in the late fall and winter.

The Oriental persimmon is native to China, where it has been grown for centuries. It is the national fruit of Japan. It came to the United States in the mid-1800s starting in California and is now grown in roughly half of the U.S. Oriental persimmon fruit ripens from late August until early December, depending on the variety and on weather conditions. Fuyu-Gaki persimmon is the most widely planted cultivar in the world. When fully ripe, this fruit will turn crimson red with a blue blush. It is also self-fruitful. Other self-fruitful varieties include Gionbo, which has very large (4 to 5") orange conical fruit, as well as Great Wall and Matsumoto. Most Oriental persimmon

trees grow about 15 feet tall and wide.

Persimmon fruits can be eaten raw or cooked, fresh or dried, and can be eaten out of hand or used in baked goods, puddings and other deserts. Low in calories and fat, this little fruit contains all kinds of phytonutrients, flavonoids and antioxidants.

In addition to being edible, persimmons have long been thought to be weather prognosticators. If you harvest the fruit of the native persimmon, find the seeds and cut them in half. (This is not easily done because they are quite slippery.) Inside each seed will be a white embryo center. They are generally shaped like a "fork," "knife" or "spoon." If you see a fork, it means a mild winter. A spoon means lots of snow (a spoon for shoveling). Finally, a knife means a cold winter ahead: It will cut like a knife!

Q & A

Q. I plant kale and rape in the spot that I will follow with tomatoes and corn since they stay green all winter. Are they a good cover crop that will add nutrients to the soil when tilled in, or do I need to plan something else to improve the soil?

A. They should do great. You can also harvest the kale before turning in the remains. Having a cover crop keeps weeds away while also enriching the soil. Other choices include vetch, rye, oats or turnips.

Q. I live out on the north side of a small mountain in the Ferndale area. I try to grow things on our 10 acres with modest success. I set out blackberries a couple of years ago beside a small running creek, but not below water level. This summer, they developed some black spots and a couple of vines died. The remainder did produce a couple of quarts. I am thinking they had some kind of rust, perhaps, because I do have oaks and cedars in our area. Should I be applying some type of dust such as rotenone? I want to be prepared for next season.

A. There are several things that could be impacting your blackberries, but from the sound of it, it isn't insects, so rotenone would not be effective. I also don't like dusts. If you are going to spray, we need to properly identify the disease (with leaf samples next year) and then find the appropriate fungicide. There is one disease called double blossom (or rosette) that affects blackberries and is not curable. It is commonly spread from wild blackberries nearby. It causes excessive thorniness on the stems and deformed, almost double blossoms–thus the common name. It can kill plants but usually does so in a slow manner. Pruning out infected canes helps. There is a rust disease that affects blackberries that is controllable. It produces very bright orange spores that can be rubbed off. Cedar apple rust does not affect blackberries, but it does affect apples. There are other leaf-spotting diseases as well as stink bug damage to the fruits.

Q. I am relatively new at trying to grow plants and trees. I have a pear tree that is young, about 3 years old now, and is still quite spindly. It produced quite a few pears this year but the trunk of the tree is very slender. I also have some plum trees that I think need fertilizing. They are older, about 10 years, and still produce, but some of the limbs have died. For both of these, should I fertilize them and if so, when?

A. Most fruit trees benefit from an application of fertilizer once or twice a year depending on their age. For young trees, broadcast a complete fertilizer (10-10-10) in early spring. You can repeat this again in June. For older trees, broadcast fertilizer around the tree every year in late March. Usually well-established trees only need one application of fertilizer a year, but watering is important for all fruit trees. In addition to fertilization, all fruit trees need to be pruned every year. For gardeners with just a few trees, late February is the ideal time to prune.

Q. During a mid-September hike, we discovered some ripe pawpaws, the first I have come across in many years. We tasted them, bringing back nice childhood memories. I saved some seeds, which I now have in my windowsill. I would like to try to grow a pawpaw tree, just as a novelty. How and when should one plant the seeds? What kind of soil is best? I do understand that this plant needs partial shade, being an understory plant. Does it have any other special requirements?

A. Unfortunately, germination is somewhat erratic on pawpaw seeds. They must go through a cool, moist period known as stratification. Get a plastic bag, fill it with moist potting soil and place the seeds inside. Then put the plastic bag in your refrigerator for two to three months. After this period you can pot the seeds, lightly covering them with soil. Be patient. You probably won't get 100 percent germination, but hope for the best. You can buy pawpaw trees from some local nurseries.

Q. When is the best time for planting fruit trees like apple, plum, cherry, pear and peach in Little Rock? Where are the nurseries or other sources for the above mentioned trees in central Arkansas?

A. Today, many fruit trees are sold as container-grown trees and can therefore be planted at any time. For best selection both in quality and variety of tree, most nurseries start getting a good selection in February. The majority of our nurseries do carry at least some fruit trees, and a few

Pawpaw

Q&A

actually specialize in them. If you can find the varieties you are looking for, November is a great time to plant them. If you have specific varieties you are looking for, you may want to visit with your local nurseryman in the fall and place an order to plant the following spring.

Q. I have two Texas Everbearing fig trees in my garden in northwest Arkansas. They are sprawled out now, and it seems that every winter they die back some and then really struggle to get any fruit. I have had them for three years now and I got a small amount of small fruits from them. How and when do you prune them? They are supposed to stand temperatures as low as 10 degrees. I really want them to do better this winter as I want more fruit!

A. Although our winters have been getting milder, northwest Arkansas often gets below 10 degrees in a typical winter. Figs are not reliably top-hardy if temperatures drop below 15 degrees, so you may experience some dieback each winter in the northern tier of the state. Even when the tops die all the way back, they will usually return from the root system each year. For that reason, add some extra mulch around the plants and don't do any pruning until spring arrives. Then assess the damage. It will not be uncommon to have plant damage even in central Arkansas if we get an excessively cold winter. The one saving grace is that figs do bear on the current season growth. I don't have great data on varietal differences, but most sources say that Celeste and Brown Turkey are the hardiest of the older varieties (Texas Everbearing is actually another name for Brown Turkey.) Two newer varieties you may want to experiment with are Alma and Hardy.

Q. In April, I planted a cutting from a fig tree in a garden area in my backyard. It has grown fast and is now over six feet and has little green figs on it. However, since the fall it has been dropping all its leaves at the bottom and the leaves further up are turning yellow and dropping. Are they supposed to do this? I remember fig trees from growing up that never seemed to drop their leaves. What's happening? When and how much do I need to prune?

A. Fig trees are deciduous, and will lose all their leaves as winter approaches. Fig trees can produce two crops of fruit, one that ripens in the summer, and another that sets in late summer through early fall and overwinters on the tree, then ripens with spring. Usually we don't get to harvest the late-season crop because of winter conditions. Get the fig tree through the winter and do whatever pruning is necessary in late February through mid-March. Figs can be somewhat winter-sensitive, so wait until spring to prune. At that tim, thinning cuts may help it open up more, and you'll need to prune to a manageable height to make picking of fruit more accessible.

Q. I'm new to Arkansas and have bought some acreage north of Batesville. It includes bottomland and a raised meadow, which I fear is a huge gravel pile covered with

a little topsoil. When I dig, I immediately hit marble-sized rocks. I have mail-ordered some pecan and chestnut trees. Both say plant in well-drained, moist soil. I'm guessing that the grassy knoll will drain well, but I don't know if it is suitable for my nut trees. By the way, the adjoining land is covered in cedar and oak trees. What do you think?

A. Just looking at soil and the lay of the land really doesn't indicate internal soil drainage. You need to dig a hole as deep as you plan to plant your trees then fill it with water until the water stands. See how long it takes for the water to drain. A well-drained soil should go down about an inch per hour. If there is still water sitting in the hole the next day, this indicates a poorly drained site, which can be a problem for fruit and nut crops. Planting, digging and then growing can be a challenge in extremely rocky soil, but much of Arkansas is in the same boat, however, it is doable. Get a soil test. Test for drainage and see if you can amend the soil in an area at least three times the width of the planting hole with compost, incorporating that with the existing soil. Give your pecan trees plenty of room to grow, since they are large trees at maturity.

Q. About 25 years ago, my mother used to empty iced tea glasses into a houseplant. In the days of using real lemons with seeds, a lemon tree popped up. After her death 22 years ago, I brought it into my house. I usually put it out every summer. I've "topped" it a couple of times because it would be 20 feet tall by now if I didn't. I'd say it's about 6 ½ ft. It has never bloomed. Why not? Are there male and female lemon trees? It has thorns on it–green and not deadly sharp.

A. How much sunlight does it get when you move it outdoors? It would need a minimum of 6 to 8 hours of sunlight per day to set flowers and bloom. A plant that large should be setting fruit. I do not know of a male lemon tree, but even if that were the case, it would have to bloom to have pollen to set on the female blossom. The fact that there are no flowers could mean the light is too low or possibly hard pruning. The plant would definitely be old enough to bloom and set fruit.

DECEMBER

Artichoke

IN MOST CASES, ARTICHOKES, beets, carrots, cauliflower, celery, Chinese cabbage, endive, lettuce, parsnips, peas, Swiss chard, escarole, arugula, bok choy, mache and radicchio can tolerate light freezes with no covering. Broccoli, Brussels sprouts, cabbage, collards, kale, kohlrabi, mustard, onions, parsley, peas, radishes, spinach, turnips, leeks, and sorrel can tolerate temperatures between 26 to 28 degrees. Temperatures below 25 degrees are dangerous territory for all vegetable plants. English peas are very hardy and the plants can tolerate heavy frost. But the blossoms will probably not produce any pods.

It is important to understand that temperature is not the only factor affecting survivorship of plants during the winter months. The stage of development, how tall the plant is, the amount of moisture in the ground and how long the cold weather lasts can all be factors. The ground is usually still warm in early December and will radiate some warmth to plants that are close to the ground. Humidity can also help protect plants from frost. Humid air holds more heat and reduces the drying effects of frost. Air movement also has an influence on frost damage.

Tender plants can be protected from a few light frosts with row covers, inverted boxes or even overturned plastic plant pots. Adding extra mulch to low-growing beets, carrots, leeks, onions, radishes and parsnips can help protect them. Light frost makes leafy greens and root vegetables sweeter, so it's worth leaving some of your kale and carrots in the ground until you're ready to use them.

To move the garden inside, consider growing sprouts to spruce up salads and sandwiches. It doesn't take much effort and you still get the reward of growing your own food. In addition, there are many herbs that you can grow in the windowsill to have fresh herbs all winter. Basil and chives are quite easy.

HARVEST

IF COOL-SEASON CROPS are not going to be grown in your garden and you have harvested all of your summer vegetables, it is time to get your garden ready for winter. Remove all plant material and dispose of it either in your compost bin or in your green recycle container. Do not put diseased, insect-infested plant materials or weeds that have gone to seed in your compost, as all disease-producing organisms or weed seeds may not be killed during the composting process. If you plan to grow your cool-season vegetables all winter, have row covers or covering on hand for really cold temperatures. Peppers, tomatoes and other summer vegetables are done for winter so remove spent foliage. Mulch the garden and continue to enjoy the harvest of cool-season crops as long as you can.

To get the most out of a garden, you can extend the growing season by sheltering plants from cold weather during the winter months. Today we have many gardeners growing their gardens year-round, harvesting greens, broccoli, cabbage, carrots and other cool-weather crops by providing the right conditions. There are many ways to lengthen the growing season and your choice depends on the amount of time and money you want to spend. Plants' protection needs will vary. Some crops can tolerate light frosts, or temperatures between 28 to 32 degrees. A hard frost typically occurs when the temperature gets below 28 degrees. Temperature alone won't determine how hard the frost is. Wind and humidity can protect plants in colder temperatures, while a clear, still, low-humidity night can lead to more damage.

Kale and Chard

Broccoli

Cabbage

There are many types of portable structures that shelter plants from drying winds and cold air. You can set individual coverings over individual plants, or you can create a tunnel to cover the entire row. Grow tunnels and hoop houses are a larger version of the cold frames, except they are usually placed over a garden bed. The supporting structure can be any size to fit over the in-ground garden or raised bed. Some people build their frame with hog wire or PVC pipes and place a clear plastic tarp over it at night. This traps solar radiation and moisture evaporating from the soil and plants. The structure is with any type of material that can be used to create a covering over the bed so the material can rest on top of the structure and have air space above the plants. It is preferable to have a design that can be closed completely at night to prevent frost damage, and opened or completely removed during the day for good air circulation. There are a variety of forms on the market now. Some work, some don't and some are easily constructed from materials around the home. An ideal covering should be lightweight, portable and reusable. They need to be anchored or heavy enough that they don't blow away on a cold, windy night. Garden catalogs are constantly promoting new ideas and products developed all with the same idea: protect plants from the wind and cold. Whatever you use, start gardening in the winter. You don't have to water as often and there are not nearly as many insect and disease pests to contend with.

PLANT OF THE MONTH

HERBS

THE USE OF HERBS DATES BACK to ancient times, but the form in which we use them has varied. It wasn't that long ago that our only familiarity with herbs were the little glass jars hanging on a wooden rack in the kitchen. Today, you may buy small bags or bundles of fresh herbs at the grocery store and at farmers markets. However, fresh cut herbs don't last long once you get them home. To make fresh herbs easier to use, why not grow your own?

Herbs may be annual or perennial plants, or grown as houseplants. Annual herbs are those that you must replant every season as they complete their life cycle in one growing season. Some are cool-season plants while others are grown in the warm season. Perennial herbs will come back for more than one year and some can last a lifetime. Some die back to the ground while others stay green year-round.

When choosing herbs for your garden, whether annual or perennial, it's best to start with the herbs you use most in your cooking–and then gradually expand. The most common annual herb grown and used today is basil. Basil is a heat lover and thrives outdoors all summer long. There are many different species of basil, from the common sweet basil to the dark purple-foliaged Purple Ruffles. There are also flavored basils including lemon, lime and cinnamon. Give basil a spot in the sun, water as needed during the summer, pinch back to prevent seed

Basil

Parsley

heads from forming and you will be rewarded with loads of fresh basil all summer.

Another common annual often planted in the vegetable garden is dill. This tall, wispy-leaved plant can be used both as foliage and seeds. Again, full sun is best.

Cilantro is an herb people either love or hate. Cilantro grows best in cool weather. Except for the far northern part of the state, it should actually overwinter outdoors quite nicely. During fall, plant cilantro to grow with winter annuals like pansies and violas. Another planting in early spring can extend your harvest season, but don't plant too late. Once the temperatures heat up in late spring, the plants will quickly bolt and go to seed. The plant then turns from cilantro to coriander, the name given to this herb when it is in seed form.

Parsley is actually a biennial. The first season it will produce foliage and the second season it blooms, sets seeds and dies. Growing parsley from seed can be challenging, but it is readily available as plants at most garden centers and is usually sold both spring and fall. Some cooks prefer the flat leaf parsley to the curly leaf, but they both grow well in the garden. Fall planting is great since they tend to be evergreen and give an excellent accent to the flowers around them.

An easy perennial herb to grow is chives. There are two main types: the more well-behaved onion chives with purple flowers and the wild garlic chives with copious white flowers, which freely reseed themselves. Plant these two easy-to-care-for plants in a sunny garden or in a container.

Rosemary is another easy herb to grow in the garden. An added benefit is that this plant is evergreen and has fairly showy blooms. There are numerous varieties of this popular herb, from prostrate forms to uprights. Hardiness of rosemary can vary by variety. Past cold winters have done some damage, but most plants have rebounded. Foliage and flowers are both used in cooking. Rosemary will not tolerate heavy, poorly drained soils, so make sure the site is well drained.

Thyme is one of the most heat and drought tolerant plants around. Like many of the other herbs mentioned, there are many types of thyme to choose from. All have small, dainty leaves and grow close to the ground, but you can get both green and variegated forms. Thyme prefers a dry site in the sun. If grown with regular overhead watering from a sprinkler system, it won't be happy. Thyme is an evergreen that thrives on neglect and is a great addition around stepping-stones, as a border to a garden or even in containers.

Sage is another evergreen, easy-care herb for the garden. There are over 900 species of salvias–some are considered more ornamental than culinary, but there are numerous common culinary salvias as well. Whether used as an ornamental or as a culinary herb, salvias have interesting aromas, textures and colors–both in flower and foliage, depending on variety. The main culinary salvia is *Salvia officinalis.* This is the sage you commonly add to the turkey stuffing at Thanksgiving. There are green-leafed varieties and variegated option, as well.

The list can go on and on. Herbs can be put into a stand-alone herb garden or mixed in with vegetables or ornamentals. They are also great in containers. If mixing with other plants, use caution when using pesticides nearby. Make sure you are grouping plants with like needs together–sun or shade, wet or dry.

Some herbs are easy to grow and sometimes get too vigorous like some of the mints. Containing them can help. Whether you are a new gardener or an experienced one, herbs are an easy addition to the garden and you can enjoy their beauty and use them in the kitchen!

Q&A

Q. Living in Hot Springs Village, I was wondering if a cold frame set up along a south facing wall, in full sun, would be warm enough to germinate seeds in late winter/early spring here, for a summer vegetable garden.

A. A cold frame on the south wall will definitely generate enough heat to start seeds and even grow cool-season vegetables all winter. The challenge will be to keep it from getting too hot. We have spells of warm weather all winter and it will get really hot inside. You will need to pay attention to the weather and vent the frame on warm, sunny days. A new trend in gardening is high tunnels or what used to be called a hoop house. You can build a small structure and cover it with clear plastic and use that to cover an existing vegetable garden to grow vegetables year-round.

Q. This year we planted our garden as usual. Most years we have average-sized tomato plants that produce a few small tomatoes. This year we have the biggest plants we have ever seen with hundreds of tomatoes that are still growing this late in the season. We have no idea what type we bought, but we would like to get them again next year. What type of tomato plants would you suggest to get these same results next season?

A. There are a lot of options when it comes to tomatoes. There are two basic types of tomato plants: determinate and indeterminate. Determinate types are often called patio or bush tomatoes. The plants are smaller, have a stronger stem and tend to produce all their tomatoes at one time and that is pretty much it for the season. This year you for sure bought an indeterminate variety. They continue to grow and produce as long as they are healthy and we are frost free. They have a weaker main stem and require staking. My personal favorite is the Traveler tomato. Other indeterminate varieties include Better Boy, Brandywine, Bradley and Early Girl. There are plenty of great tomato varieties out there, but you definitely want an indeterminate variety if you want to repeat your long harvest season.

Q. My dwarf Meyer lemon tree is losing its leaves. It also has new growth. I water it once a week and I fertilize it with Miracle Grow every three months. What am I doing wrong?

A. There are many factors that could be in play. If you just recently moved it inside, it could be shedding leaves due to a change in conditions. The later you wait to move them inside, the more shock of transplant the plant will experience, which can lead to shedding leaves. If the tree is inside year-round, it may not be getting enough light. Winter tends to be the driest season indoors and houseplants struggle with the lack of humidity. Pot size, plant size, the temperature indoors and how much light it receives can all be factors with how often it needs to be watered and how happy it is indoors. I assume the pot has a drainage hole for excess water to flow out, but make sure it is not staying too wet. The more sunlight the plant can get, the better. I would keep it alive for the winter and move it outdoors next spring, which should lead to a rebound in growth.

Q & A

Q. My persimmon tree did not fruit this year. I have two males and one female persimmon all in close proximity to one another, and even in the severe drought years, we had fruit–lots of it. All my other trees, especially my walnut, over-produced this year. I have talked with several other folks who have persimmons and all but one have said the same thing. The one exception said that he had fruit, but very, very little, and he also found that strange. What gives?

A. Did you have an exceptionally heavy crop last year? Persimmons can go through what is known as alternate bearing: a heavy crop one year and little to none the next. It is also possible your tree got hit by a late frost, which could have damaged the blooms. Not much can be done at this point, but let's hope for a better crop next year.

Q. I've been trying to grow Italian parsley in a pot to keep indoors during winter, and it will grow well for a few months and then the leaves start to wilt and curl up. I'm an experienced gardener so I don't over water, and I use a professional potting mix that contains fertilizer, so I don't fertilize at all. One variable here is that I allowed the Black Swallowtail caterpillars to feast on it and they pruned it down to the soil level, but it has grown back again. Any suggestions?

A. You would have been much better off planting the parsley outdoors than inside. It is a tad late to get it established outside, but if you can find a nursery still selling it, give it a try. Parsley thrives in cool weather. I usually plant it along with my pansies and violas. It is a biennial, meaning it will only live for two seasons before blooming, setting seed and dying. The warm indoor conditions with low light and low humidity will make it difficult to grow. For best luck, give it a bright location and the coolest spot you can find inside. Do not attempt to plant your struggling plant outside now, since it would not be acclimated to the cold, and would promptly die.

Q. We have quite a few herbs still growing in our garden now. What can you do with chives at this time of year? What about sage, rosemary and thyme? I even have some basil that is still producing. Can you dry them or is it better to freeze them?

A. Chives, sage, rosemary and thyme are perennial herbs, while basil is an annual. Harvest all of the basil prior to a killing frost and use it fresh or dried. Or you can put it into an ice cube tray, cover it with water and freeze the leaves inside to add to soups, stews and sauces. Depending on where you live in the state, chives can stay green in the winter or die back. If yours die back, then cutting them prior to a freeze is advisable. Again, fresh, dried or frozen will work. For thyme, sage and rosemary, harvest as needed throughout the winter. Just don't get carried away and cut too much, as they won't be putting on much new growth during the winter months. Tip: Rosemary is being sold now for the holidays in topiary tree and wreath forms. Leave these plants outdoors, as they die quickly inside. If the temperatures are predicted to get extremely low–below 28 degrees–you may want to move these potted rosemary plants into a garage or storage building temporarily. While rosemary is quite hardy through most of the state, container plants are less so because of limited roots, plus the soil in the containers gets colder than soil in the ground.

Q. Last Christmas I purchased a rosemary bush in the shape of a Christmas tree for the holidays. I planted it in a planter and put it by my front door (outside) for a sunny location. The tag said it can stay outdoors to 10 degrees. After one hard frost, it began to look dead and it did not recover. I did not leave it out in temperatures below 20 degrees so I am disappointed that I killed it. I would like to try again this year if there is hope. Any pointers?

A. Rosemary is a hardy plant, and you did the right thing by upgrading the container. Most of the pots they come in are fairly small and elevated plants are more sensitive to cold than those planted in the ground or in larger containers. Make sure the soil does not get too wet, since that can be a death knell as well. I have used them in the past for decoration, but moved them behind other shrubs or into the garage when the temperature is well below freezing. Established plants are much tougher than new ones.

Q. I just purchased a rosemary plant that is being sold for Christmas in topiary form. Is this plant good to cook with? This is the reason I purchased it. I have heard it is best to leave it outdoors, but I put it in my store room, as it is cool in there. Also, can it be repotted as it grows?

A. These Christmas tree sheared rosemary plants are an excellent plant to cook with. Prune judiciously to keep the shape, but by all means use it. Repot it as needed. It can also be planted in the ground outdoors this spring. Rosemary plants usually thrive in our gardens, but in that small container you are wise to protect it during these cold days. Inside a heated house, the lack of humidity, constant heat and low light often prove fatal for rosemary plants within a few weeks. If you can keep it cool and in bright light, it should fare well.

Rosemary

Q & A

Q. We moved into our house in May and found we have grapevines. The type is Catawba, and my question deals with pruning. What is the best time to prune, and how much should I prune them back? I also have a lot of blackberry vines–does the same apply to them?

A. Pruning grapes differs tremendously from pruning blackberries. Grapevines should be pruned every year in late February. How old the vines are will determine how much to prune. You start by counting buds on the existing vines, starting where the vines begin to branch out (we call these the arms). Each bud you leave on the vines should result in a cluster of grapes. On young vines, you should leave about 10 to 15 buds. You will be removing more than 50 percent of the plant. Many gardeners think they are hurting the plant by pruning this much, but if you leave too many buds, the vines won't have enough energy to ripen that many grapes, resulting in clusters that ripen a grape at a time. A mature grapevine can handle up to 60 buds. Depending on your trellising system, you can leave 2 to 4 arms on the vines and divide the buds between them. Blackberry pruning is done during the growing season. After you harvest the blackberries in the summer, thin out the old canes, since the old canes die after they bear fruit. The key is to get the old canes out as soon after production as possible to make way for the new canes. The canes that are left will produce the fruit for next season. For the remainder of the summer, keep the new canes pruned back to a height of 4 to 5 feet, so the canes will branch but keep the fruit within easy picking reach next summer.

Q. I have two miniature citrus plants, an orange and another, lemon or tangerine, not sure. They are 4 or more years old, but have never bloomed. I take them outside on a carport or patio during the summer and they thrive, but do not bloom. Is there something I can do to help them?

A. Citrus plants need bright light year round to do best. They may also have not come of age yet. Give them a bright spot indoors and out, fertilize while outside and avoid any significant pruning, which may interfere with bloom.

Q. I have always saved the tops of pineapple and planted them in a pot. I have grown nice plants. Two years ago, I started one, and this year I have a pineapple! Now I don't know what to do with it. Should I cut it off and replant the top?

A. Pot-grown pineapples rarely achieve the size of the pineapples at the supermarket, but they are fun to grow and a novelty. Let it mature and you can eat the fruit regardless of the size and replant the top. Keep in mind that once a pineapple plant produces a fruit, the mother plant will die. But there should be daughter plants at the base to take its place. Pineapples are bromeliads and can produce a fruit when the plant is 2 years of age or older. For future reference, put the plant inside a large plastic bag and stick an apple or two in with it to aid in fruit set when the plant is the appropriate age and size. Apples give off ethylene gas, which should encourage the plant to produce a fruit. Leave the plant sealed up with the apples for several days. Then discard the apples and give the pineapple plant full sun and see what happens.

RECIPES

Stuffed Peppadew Peppers

This appetizer can be made to feed as many people as you would like. Peppadew peppers are available in the olive bars at many grocery stores. They come most commonly in red, but you can find yellow and orange varieties, too.

Ingredients:
1 lb pork sausage, browned and drained of fat
1 8 oz package softened cream cheese
½ tsp garlic powder
½ cup grated cheese of choice
(I have used sharp cheddar, feta and Italian blend)
Peppadew peppers

Mix everything but the peppers.

Drain the peppers if they still have liquid around them, and then fill with mixture. For smaller batches, use a narrow spoon to fill. Fill a baking dish with them stacked side by side. A tight fit is good because it keeps the filling upright when it is heating up.

Once filled, lightly sprinkle with finely grated Parmesan cheese and bake in a 350-degree oven for 20 minutes or until lightly brown.

Suggested: Pulse the filling a few times in a food processor to get a smoother finish if making a lot for later piping the filling into the peppadews.

Serve warm or at room temperature.

Roasted Baby Bok Choy

Ingredients:
4 heads baby bok choy (1 ¼ lbs), leaves separated
4 tsp olive oil
1-2 cloves garlic, minced
(depending on how much you like garlic)
¼ tsp salt
½ tsp lemon zest, freshly grated
1 tbsp lemon juice
½ tsp fresh tarragon, chopped or ¾ tsp dried
1 tsp mirin (*see Note)
freshly ground pepper to taste

Preheat oven to 450 degrees. Toss bok choy, oil, garlic and salt, then spread on a cookie sheet. Roast on lowest rack, stirring twice until wilted and tender-crisp, about 6 minutes. Whisk lemon zest and juice, tarragon, mirin and pepper in a small bowl. Drizzle over the roasted bok choy immediately upon removal from the oven. Serve.

***Note:** Mirin is a low-alcohol rice wine used in Japanese cooking. I can find it at my grocery store with the Asian or gourmet ingredients. If you can't find it, substitute with an equal portion of sherry or white wine with a pinch of sugar.

Grilled Vegetable Salad

Ingredients:
Use whatever vegetables on hand or preferred from the following list:
Asparagus
Onions
Squash–yellow or zucchini
Peppers–hot or sweet
Eggplant
Mushrooms
Tomatoes

Slice vegetables and toss with Greek seasoning, garlic powder, salt, pepper and olive oil.

Grill the vegetables on a medium to hot grill using grill pan, turning occasionally. When slightly charred, remove to a bowl and sprinkle with feta, chopped basil and a drizzle of balsamic vinegar.

Can be eaten hot as a side dish, or chilled as a cold salad.

Kale and Quinoa Pilaf

Ingredients:
2 cups salted water
1 cup quinoa
1 bunch kale, washed and chopped
1 lemon, zested and juiced
2 green onions sliced fine, both green and whites
1 tsp sesame oil
3 tbsp pine nuts, toasted
¼ cup goat cheese, crumbled
salt and pepper

Bring water to a boil in a covered pot. Add quinoa. Cover and lower heat. Let simmer for 10 minutes then top with kale and re-cover. Simmer 5 minutes. Turn off heat and allow mixture to steam for 5 minutes. If there is still water, cook until there is no water in pot.

While quinoa is cooking, place lemon juice, green onions, sesame oil, pine nuts and goat cheese in a large serving bowl and set aside.

When quinoa is fully cooked, fluff with fork. Add cooked quinoa and kale to top of the ingredients in bowl and toss to combine.

Season pilaf with salt and pepper to taste. This dish can be eaten hot or at room temperature.

Zucchini Carpaccio

Ingredients:
1 lb zucchini
2 tbsp extra virgin olive oil
2 lemons
1 tsp pickled capers
sprig fresh thyme
4-6 pitted black olives
crushed red pepper
salt and pepper

Wash and trim zucchini. Slice zucchini evenly and paper-thin. Place zucchini slices in a circular pattern, slightly overlapping, on a large, round plate. Spray or sprinkle one juiced lemon over zucchini slices. Let rest for 15 minutes to soften.

Remove capers and dry with a paper towel. Slice olives (should provide 4-6 slices per olive). Mince thyme and capers together. Combine thyme, capers, sliced olives, ½ juiced lemon, olive oil, dash of salt and 2 tbsp warm water. For a dense sauce, beat well with fork.

Pour prepared sauce over sliced zucchini and lightly sprinkle with freshly grated black pepper. Refrigerate for 15 minutes.

Thinly slice remaining ½ lemon. Garnish zucchini with lemon slices and red peppers sprinkled throughout.

Serve slightly chilled.

Squash Casserole

Ingredients:
½ large onion, diced
1-2 cloves of garlic, minced
1 jalapeno, diced
4 cups yellow squash thinly sliced
2 eggs
1 cup shredded cheese
1 tbsp garlic chili paste or hot sauce
salt and pepper
dash of chili powder
1 cup buttery round crackers, crushed

Preheat oven to 350 degrees. Prepare casserole dish with non-stick cooking spray.

Sauté onion, garlic and jalapeno in olive oil until soft. Add squash and continue to sauté 5 minutes.

In a separate bowl, mix eggs, cheese, garlic chili paste, salt, pepper and chili powder. Add sautéed vegetables to egg mixture. Pour mixture into prepared casserole dish and sprinkle with crushed crackers.

Bake 20-30 minutes, or until top is browned. Serve.

Spicy Asparagus Strata

Ingredients:

3 scallions or 2 shallots, diced
8 oz asparagus, trimmed and cut into 1-inch pieces (about 2 cups)
1 cup mushrooms, sliced
6 large eggs
1 ½ cups half-and-half
1 tsp kosher salt
½ tsp cumin
¼ tsp ground black pepper
Fresh ground nutmeg
1 loaf French bread, sliced ½-inch thick (can substitute sandwich bread)
1 ½ cups shredded cheese
½ cup pickled jalapenos, drained and coarsely chopped
½ cup fresh cilantro leaves, chopped plus more for garnish

Butter 9-by-11-inch baking dish and set aside. Sauté scallions/shallots for 1 minute in olive oil. Add asparagus, mushrooms and cook until asparagus are bright green and soft, or 2-3 minutes. Remove from heat.

Whisk eggs, half-and-half, salt, cumin, nutmeg and pepper in a large bowl until combined. Arrange half of the bread in bottom of prepared dish. Sprinkle half asparagus, mushroom and onion mix, then half each of jalapenos, cilantro and cheese. Pour it over the egg mixture. Repeat layering with remaining bread, vegetable mix, jalapenos, cilantro and cheese. Pour remaining egg mixture over top.

Push to ensure bread is submerged in egg custard. Cover with plastic wrap and place in refrigerator for 1 to 12 hours (or overnight).

Heat oven to 325 degrees. Let strata sit at room temperature while oven heats, at least 20 minutes.

Bake in middle rack until puffed and edges pull away slightly, about 40-45 minutes. Cool 5 minutes before serving. Serve with cilantro, sour cream and avocado, as desired.

Orzo Salad with Vegetables and Feta

Ingredients:
1½ cup orzo (rice-shaped pasta)
½ lb sugar snap peas
2 medium tomatoes
(or a dozen cherry tomatoes, halved)
6 scallions, thinly sliced
1 cup flat leafed parsley, chopped
1/3 cup feta, crumbled

For dressing: Blend ingredients for dressing until emulsified.
½ garlic clove
2 tablespoons fresh lemon juice
¼ cup flat leaved parlsey
2 tsp fresh oregano, minced
freshly ground pepper
¼ cup olive oil

Cook orzo in a large pot of boiling water until al dente. Add snap peas to the cooking water for 15 seconds. Drain pasta and peas, cool for 5 minutes. Stir in feta, tomatoes, scallions and parsley.

Add dressing and toss.

This makes a great side dish and can be served warm or cold. To make it a meal, add grilled shrimp or chicken.

Butternut Squash Soup

Ingredients:
1 tbsp olive oil
1 tbsp unsalted butter
1 medium onion, chopped
1-3 cloves garlic, chopped
2 ½ lb butternut squash, peeled, seeded and cubed
½ Granny Smith apple, peeled, cored and diced
4 cups chicken broth
1 ½ tsp salt
½ tsp fresh thyme, chopped
Red pepper flakes to taste
¼ tsp fresh ground pepper

Sauté onion in olive oil for approximately 5 minutes or until soft. Add butter, squash and apple, sauté 5 minutes. Add remaining ingredients and bring to a boil. Reduce heat to simmer, cover and cook until squash is tender, about 20 minutes. Remove from heat. Use an immersion blender to blend. Serve immediately or refrigerate for up to three days.

*Butternut squash can be substituted with pumpkin puree or fresh pumpkin.

Meal in a Pumpkin

Ingredients:
1 medium pumpkin
1½ lb ground meat (beef, turkey or lamb)
1 medium onion, diced
1 bell pepper, diced
2 cloves garlic, diced
¾ cup mushrooms, sliced
1 can diced tomatoes
2 tbsp soy sauce
1 tbsp brown sugar
1 tbsp ketchup
2 cups cooked rice

Cut off top of pumpkin and thoroughly clean out pulp and seeds.

Preheat oven to 350 degrees.

In a large skillet, sauté onions, peppers, garlic and mushrooms in olive oil until tender. Add meat and brown. Drain drippings from skillet. Add tomatoes, soy sauce, brown sugar and ketchup. Simmer 10 minutes, stirring occasionally. Add cooked rice and stir. Spoon mixture into cleaned pumpkin shell. Replace pumpkin top and place entire pumpkin, with filling, on a baking sheet. Bake 1 hour or until inside meat of the pumpkin is tender. Put pumpkin on a plate. Remove pumpkin lid and serve.

About the author

JANET CARSON

Janet Carson is the statewide Consumer Horticulture Specialist and Arkansas Master Gardener Coordinator for the University of Arkansas Division of Agriculture Cooperative Extension Service. She has her BS and MS degrees from the University of Arkansas, Fayetteville.

Janet began her career as a county agent in Pulaski County covering all aspects of horticulture. She began the Arkansas Master Gardener program with three other counties in 1980. Upon completion of her Masters Janet moved to the state extension office to take on the role of statewide horticulture specialist, and helped expand the Master Gardener program throughout the state.

In addition to her Master Gardener work, she is a featured speaker at horticulture events across the state and throughout the south. She has an extensive media program with weekly columns in the *Arkansas Democrat-Gazette* on Saturdays and monthly columns in *Arkansas Living* and *Arkansas Gardener* magazines. She also tapes weekly television spots from Garvan Woodland Gardens in Hot Springs.

She was the 2003 recipient of the John White Award for Excellence in Extension Education and received the 2010 Extension Educator Award from the American Society for Horticultural Science. Her first book *In the Garden* was published in 2010 by the *Arkansas Democrat-Gazette.*

Janet is married with two grown children and four dogs.